1978

SUICIDE
AND
MORALITY

SUICIDE
AND
MORALITY

THE THEORIES OF PLATO, AQUINAS AND KANT
AND THEIR RELEVANCE FOR SUICIDOLOGY

By
DAVID NOVAK

SCHOLARS STUDIES PRESS Inc.
NEW YORK, NEW YORK

Library of Congress Cataloging in Publication Data

Novak, David, 1941-
 Suicide and morality.

 A revision of the author's thesis, Georgetown
University, 1971.
  Bibliography: p.
  1. Suicide. 2. Plato—Ethics. 3. Thomas Aquinas,
Saint, 1225?-1274—Ethics. 4. Kant, Immanuel, 1724-
1804—Ethics. I. Title.
BD445.N68 1975   179'.7   75-37543

To the memory of

C. A., M. Z., J. F. and I. B. P.

My bretheren are distant from me,
    and my friends are wholly estranged.
My kinfolk have abandoned me,
    and my fellows have forgotten me.

Job 19:13-14

TABLE OF CONTENTS

PREFACE

This book is a slight reworking of my doctoral dissertation which I submitted to the faculty of Georgetown University in March, 1971. Here I have tried to make it somewhat less technical and, therefore, of greater interest to a wider readership.

The book is a philosophical reflection on the moral problem of suicide. I believe my chief reason for writing it should be stated.

During the years of my graduate work in philosophy (1966-1969) I served as Jewish chaplain to St. Elizabeths Hospital, National Institute of Mental Health in Washington, D.C. In the course of my rabbinate there I came into close personal contact with many suicidal patients. Simultaneously, I was in close personal contact with some of the people, psychiatrists, psychologists, social workers, who were trying to help them. In my graduate program in philosophy my field of specialization was ethics.

At the hospital we had frequent meetings where we discussed approaches to treatment. At the university we discussed approaches to ethics. Eventually I came to realize that the world of the hospital and the world of the university were not separate and unrelated but were both concerned with human beings as persons. However, both approaches were incomplete. At the hospital my colleagues had much experience in dealing with persons in depth, but their discussions revealed a lack of comprehensive theory which would give overall direction to their action. At the university, on the other hand, my colleagues had little experience in dealing with persons in depth, but they were skilled in developing theories for human action.

Having one foot in each world, so to speak, I became fascinated with the idea of combining both perspectives, namely, conceptualizing my therapeutic experience and schematizing my philosophical concepts. I decided that it would be highly worthwhile to bring about greater communication between psychotherapy and philosophy, for both deal with human beings as persons. My doctoral dissertation provided the opportunity for me to do so.

Most of this study was written during the summer and fall of 1970 in Oklahoma City, Oklahoma where I served as a rabbi. I am grateful for the comparative leisure of that year.

My thanks are due to my thesis mentor and teacher, Professor Germain G. Grisez who has the gift of combining together criticism and encouragement to his students. The staffs of the libraries of the University of Oklahoma, St. Louis University and the Library of Congress were most helpful in supplying me with necessary materials for my research. Conversations with the following friends and colleagues were of great help in clarifying my thinking on numerous questions: Drs. J. A. Farrell, A. C. Gullattee, Julian Jurand, Mauris Platkin, Warren Poland, and Mrs. M. H. Mills. My wife, Melva, and my late father-in-law, Dr. Charles I. Ziman helped me greatly in the preparation of the manuscript.

Lastly, this work is dedicated to the memory of four of my patient friends who chose their own deaths. All of them believed themselves to be abandoned. Perhaps my interest in suicide prevention is motivated by my conscience which some day, I believe, will have to answer whether I too did not abandon them.

David Novak

Baltimore, Maryland
November, 1974

CHAPTER I

INTRODUCTION

The problem of suicide has intrigued thoughtful persons throughout history because it involves many significant human issues, and because it is an option always open to virtually everyone. Therefore, no normative ethics can be considered either profound or complete unless it deals with suicide. History bears out this point. There has hardly been a major ethical philosophy which has not dealt with suicide in one way or another. In the history of philosophy there have been arguments justifying suicide, arguments that its moral value is contingent on circumstance, and arguments for the prohibition of it as immoral.

In this study I shall consider three of the strongest and most carefully developed philosophical arguments for the prohibition of suicide: the arguments proposed by Plato, Aquinas and Kant. I intend to examine the arguments these philosophers put forward to investigate how these arguments are rooted in their general theories of human nature and action. I consider these three arguments to be models of philosophical reflection on the problem of suicide.

Plato, Aquinas and Kant agree that suicide is an immoral act. However, my inclusion of them in this study is also justified by further similarities. First, a threefold approach is common to their treatments of the problem. All of them deal with suicide in the context of three basic human relationships: the relationship of a person with himself, the relationship of a person with society, and the relationship of a person with God. The prohibition of suicide is explained by reference to this threefold structure. All three philosophers see suicide as fundamentally inconsistent with the nature of these three relationships. The difference in the ways these philosophers developed their prohibitions of suicide is due to differences in their philosophical anthropologies, their social philosophies, and their philosophical theologies. In other words, all of them had the task of grounding their specific ethical judgments that suicide is immoral in their general metaphysical principles.

Second, Plato, Aquinas and Kant recognized a history of discourse about suicide. All of them deal with antecedent discussions of the problem and its related issues. Plato begins his own treatment of suicide by presenting it as a problem received from earlier Pythagorean and Orphic Philosophy. Two of the authorities upon whom Aquinas leans, Aristotle and Augustine, had condemned suicide for widely different reasons. Aquinas simply repeats Aristotle's prohibition of suicide, although other related texts will show that he did not accept many of the conclusions one could draw from Aristotle. Aquinas actually presents Augustine's statement prohibiting suicide verbatim; however, Aquinas, by introducing the principle of natural inclination, provides a new grounding for Augustine's prohibition of suicide. Kant was well aware of the Stoic permission of suicide. He had to refute it inasmuch as it claimed to be grounded in respect for human dignity, while Kant held that suicide is prohibited by respect for human dignity. Furthermore, Kant's metaphysics would not allow him to base his moral judgments on earlier considerations of natural inclination; he, therefore, had to explicitly deny natural inclination as a ground for the prohibition of suicide.

In the, third place, Plato, Aquinas and Kant deal with suicide in a framework of objective moral principles. The prohibition of suicide for all of them is a *specific* ethical judgment. Now a specific judgment stands midway between a general principle and a particular decision, that is, it is neither its own ground nor its own application. All of them judge suicide immoral on the basis of general principles about human nature. These principles are prior to considerations of suicide as a human act. None of them considers the judgment that suicide is immoral to be identical with the decision of a particular person to refrain from committing suicide. Judgment must precede decision. Now a judgment that a specific group of human acts is immoral is only possible if based upon a theory of human nature. Only by affirming what is essentially and immutably human can one then judge that a species of acts is immoral because it contradicts human nature. Human nature is the ground of specific moral judgment. Without this grounding in human nature, the only frame of reference left for moral judgment is the situation of the particular act. However, since situations are variable they cannot be the ground for the moral judgment of a species of acts. Each individual act, then, is relative to the particular situation in which it happens to be found. In this type of "situation ethics" it is impossible to make any consistent distinction between a specific moral judgment and a particular moral decision.

Neither Plato nor Aquinas nor Kant can be considered a "situationist" in the currently accepted sense. All three of them base their specific judgments that suicide is immoral on general principles. Each one's ethics may be called objective. In Plato the objective principle of responsibility is the practical meaning of the human person's status as an *intelligence* in the world. In Aquinas the objective principle of natural inclination is the practical meaning of the human person's status as a *being* in the world. In Kant the objective principle of respect is the practical meaning of the human status as a *person* in the world. In each of the three theories, the general objective state is presupposed by the specific ethical judgment of any particular, subjective, situation. Thus ethical judgments are the link between ethically significant principles and ethically significant situations.

Because of this common ethical objectivity, the prohibitions of suicide by Plato, Aquinas and Kant could not be acceptable to those philosophers who would call themselves "empiricists" nor to those philosophers who would call themselves "existentialists", for these two philosophical outlooks agree in rejecting the validity of metaphysics. Both see experience as the irreducible ground for all ethical judgments inasmuch as the notion of human nature is a metaphysical notion they reject a priori. The denial that there is a specific human nature entails the denial that there can be specific moral judgments. Therefore, empiricists and existentialists are forced by their own assumptions to challenge the designation of any class of human acts as specifically immoral. Indeed, contemporary "situation ethics" seems to have provided a common approach to moral questions for many empiricists and existentialists.

Therefore, any philosophical treatment of the positions of Plato, Aquinas and Kant must take into consideration the situationist objections to their specific prohibitions of suicide. In the Aquinas section I will deal with them at greatest length, because his principle of natural inclination seems to be easily reducible to experience. There I will deal with the objections raised by Sidney Hook, and by Hume before him. In the Plato section the objections concern the internal consistency of his own arguments. In the Kant section I will take into consideration certain empiricist objections to the sufficiency of the categorical imperative for all ethical decisions. Therefore, the full explication of the respective prohibitions will have to resolve some major problems, internal as regards consistency, external as regards sufficiency. Some of these problems are dealt with by the philosophers themselves: by Plato in terms of the antithesis inherent in dialectic; by Aquinas in the objections he raises at the beginning of every article in the *Summa Theologica;* and by Kant in the "casuistical questions" he raises at the end of every section of the *Metaphysic of Morals.* Moreover, anticipations of the objections of later philosophers will be brought in when they are relevant.

The procedure in examining the treatments of suicide and morality in Plato, Aquinas and Kant will be as follows.

The first task will be to present their direct arguments for the prohibition of suicide in terms of the issues they themselves explicitly raise. At this level I will analyze the terminology each philosopher employs and the logical structure of his argument. Particular philological considerations will be taken up in the notes, unless the original meaning of a term is crucial for the understanding of the argument itself. I will also include appropriate comments made in the exegetical literature on the text itself.

The second task will be to see how the argument is grounded in the whole philosophical approach of each philosopher. I will examine and discuss the key terms in the argument and their use in the more general discussions of the philosopher will be discussed. Here, too, I will refer to the relevant insights of various exegetes.

The third task will be to deal with objections to both the arguments themselves and to the more general principles upon which they are based, where these more general objections directly affect the arguments against suicide. These objections are twofold, those raised by the philosophers themselves and those raised by other philosophers. Here I will try to show how these philosophers either explicitly handled these objections, or how these objections might be handled in terms of possible answers which might be derived from their general philosophical discussions.

All of what I have outlined so far has been on the level of analysis of philosophical arguments. However, the general objection could be raised whether analysis of the philosophical arguments of others is itself philosophy. Surely philosophy should involve some first-hand reflection, that is, it should be more than textual exegesis. In other words, some personal conclusions should be arrived at over and above the description of the conclusions of others. Philosophy has both an analytical and a synthetic function. For the most part, I have reserved my effort at synthesis for the concluding chapter.

In the conclusion I will deal with two problems. First, any reflection on suicide cannot be taken seriously today unless it takes into direct consideration the findings of the social sciences, especially sociology and psychology. We know a good deal more about suicide today than was known in the days of Plato, Aquinas or Kant. The social sciences have revolutionized our understanding of the human person. Therefore, since synthesis succeeds analysis in the sequence of understanding, I must attempt to determine whether a viable synthesis of the views that have been analyzed is possible today. At first glance, it seems as though Plato, Aquinas and Kant are not talking about the same thing as Durkheim, Freud, and their successors in sociology and psychology. In the conclusion I will argue that although we have discovered many new attributes of suicide, nevertheless, in essence, both philosophy and sociology and psychology are talking about the same thing. I will try to show that just as philosophy cannot ignore the empirical perspective developed by the social sciences, neither should the social sciences ignore the metaphysical perspective developed by philosophy. Hence I must explicate the precondition for synthesis; in the specific question of suicide such explication means showing that the psychotherapeutic treatment of the suicidal person, if it is to be an intelligent course of human action, requires both empirical and philosophical perspectives.

In the second part of the conclusion I will try to synthesize a unified position which will incorporate some of the conclusions of the analysis of the previous chapters. I will use the threefold structure of relationships, previously used for descriptive purposes, for some constructive purposes. In other words, I believe that any adequate understanding of suicide involves a theory of what constitutes a relationship with oneself, a theory of what constitutes a relationship with society, and a theory of what constitutes a relationship with that which transcends his life. Therefore, I will attempt very briefly to select the one theory I believe best understands each of these respective relationships. I will employ three criteria for selection. First, I will look for the theory most immediately intelligible, that is, the theory having the fewest presuppositions. Secondly, I will look for the theory which incorporates the greatest number of pertinent issues involved in the specific relationship. Thirdly, I will look for the theory which is most directly applicable to the empirical findings of sociology and psychology. Since I see psychotherapy as the bridge between the descriptive perspective of the social sciences and the reflective perspective of philosophy, the third criterion will be the relevance of theory to the psychotherapeutic treatment of the suicidal person.

The conclusion will be incomplete and sketchy; a fuller elaboration would require a separate analysis of various theories of psychotherapy in general and of the psychotherapeutic understanding of suicide in particular and much empirical data as well. I have chosen to limit the purview of this study by excluding such further studies. If I have outlined some methodological considerations and demonstrated the practical need for a unified understanding of suicide, then I shall have done something of value over and above my analysis of the various arguments.

CHAPTER II

SUICIDE AND HUMAN RESPONSIBILITY IN PLATO

Introduction

The morality of suicide is one of the most complicated problems Plato faced in the development of his philosophical ethics. This chapter will concentrate on his two treatments of the problem: the first in the *Phaedo* 61C-63C; the second in the *Laws* 873C-D. These texts have been of considerable interest to both classical philologists and philosophers; but my concern is with the philosophical arguments they either contain or presuppose concerning the immorality of suicide. I can not deal with any exclusively textual problems here. I will, rather, rely on the conclusions of recognized Platonic scholars. For example, when I allude to "Socrates" I mean the main character in *Plato's* early and middle dialogues. To become involved in questions of the actual historical relationship between Socrates and his pupil, Plato would take us too far afield. The notes will indicate the exegetical literature where these textual problems and related historical questions are discussed at length.

I will consider the arguments against suicide from the *Phaedo* first, then those from the *Laws*. However, the fact that the arguments from the *Phaedo* are developed in a dialectic, whereas those from the *Laws* are presented in statutory form, will call for two different methods of interpretation. In dealing with the *Phaedo* my presentation will be primarily a commentary. The problems of interpretation lie for the most part within the text. My task is to determine the meaning *therein*. In dealing with the *Laws*, I will have to determine which philosophical questions underly the statute about suicide; then I will have to discover treatments of these questions elsewhere in Plato's earlier writings. The problem here is to determine

7

the meaning underlying the text. As we shall see, suicide is discussed in a different context in the *Phaedo* than in the *Laws*. In the *Phaedo* suicide is seen as a problem involved in man's relationship with himself as an embodied soul, then as a problem involved in man's relationship with the gods. In the *Laws,* suicide is seen as a problem involved in man's relationship with society to which he belongs as a participant in a rational order, then as a problem involved in his relationship with the gods. Thus the method of presentation, and to a certain extent the subject matter as well, is different in the two texts. These differences call for a difference in interpretation. That is why the two texts must be treated separately. However, I will also attempt to show that the statute in the *Laws* results from a deeper development of principles first presented in the *Phaedo,* in the *Republic,* and in the *Timaeus.*

2. *Phaedo 61C-63C.*

The *Phaedo* text contains many exegetical problems which have been debated by scholars since Hellenistic times. A philosopher's means of literary expression will reflect his difficulty in reaching the philosophical goal toward which he is struggling. The difficulty of the *Phaedo* text surely reflects how deeply Plato struggled with the problem of suicide. Therefore, Plato's immediate meaning must be ascertained in particular before the larger philosophical questions involved in suicide can be analyzed. Since the points developed in the *Phaedo* are presented as suppositions in a closely constructed dialectic, it would be a mistake, I believe, to abstract a complete position from the actual dialectic. It is, therefore, the intention of this section of the chapter to present a translation of *Phaedo* 61C-63C in the most intelligible way possible, and then comment on it so that the text might appear as one coherent dialectical argument.

The methodological presupposition of coherency in the text itself is essential to the overall philosophical objective. If the argument is not fundamentally coherent, if Plato is merely mouthing a traditional doctrine without being able to fathom its intelligibility, then it does not admit of philosophical analysis. There are a number of scholars who believe that such is indeed the case. One author argues that Plato is expressing his own unresolved feelings on suicide. For this reason he had to express the problem and its solution in terms of authoritative Pythagorean doctrines without the usual Socratic scrutiny.[1] Another author believes the meaning of this section of the *Phaedo* is essentially mythological.[2] Earlier, both Plotinus and Augustine simply repeated the Platonic ban on suicide without attempting any analysis of its intelligibility.[3] However, my presentation will assume that the meaning of the text is neither inconsistent nor esoteric; and this assumption will be justified philosophically, not philologically.

Socrates mentions the prohibition of suicide at the very end of his message to Evenus, a member of the religious circle which included Cebes, who becomes Socrates interlocutor on this question. These men, because of their devotion to Pythagorean religious philosophy, are interested in the affinities in Socrates' teaching. Socrates: "So tell Evenus that, Cebes, and bid him farewell, and tell him, if he is rational, to come after me as soon as possible." (61C) Socrates believes that the reception of his advice depends on whether Evenus is rational, namely, whether he is in deliberate control of his actions. Elsewhere in the *Phaedo* this quality is made the mark of a philosopher.[4] This, then, is the force of Socrates' rhetorical question, "Is not Evenus a philosopher?" Only a philosopher would be concerned with these matters in the way Socrates is dealing with them.

Socrates then generalizes: "So Evenus will take my advice, and so will every man who is rightly involved in this question. Yet, perhaps, he will not do violence to himself for they say that is not permitted." The use of the tentative "perhaps" introduces the moral dilemma of suicide, especially for Evenus or any true philosopher. The implication of Socrates' "follow me" would seem to permit suicide. It has imperative force in this context. And yet, "they say it is not permitted."[5] It is this paradox, then, which Cebes catches and throws back at Socrates. The bearing of "perhaps" is not upon what Evenus will do as a random individual but what he will do as a philosopher. The problem becomes the reconciliation of philosophy and the inherited moral tradition which manifests itself in an unavoidable life choice, a life choice which philosophers will more likely have to make.

Cebes retorts: "How can you say this, Socrates, but still hold that the philosopher is to follow after the dying." (61D) Being confronted with this retort, Socrates once again refers to the traditional authority of the ban on suicide, that of the Pythagorean teacher, Philolaus. But Cebes is not interested in arguments from authority and myths about the other world. He is persistent in following the theme.

"Why indeed then do they say that it is not permitted to kill oneself, Socrates? I heard Philolaus, when he dwelt among us, say just what you said, and I have heard it from some others too, that this is not to be done; but I never heard anyone say anything definite about it."

The issue is unavoidable.

Now the first point in the argument is introduced. This particular passage offers the greatest philological problems in the entire "suicide text" of the *Phaedo*. There has been considerable debate throughout the ages as to its authentic meaning. The literature is quite extensive. The translation I use is that of R. S. Bluck.[6]

. . . and yet maybe it will seem surprizing to you that while this alone of all things admits of no qualifications and it *never* happens (as with everything else) that death is preferable to life for man only on *some* occasions and *some* cases, yet nevertheless—it seems surprising to you perhaps—these human beings, for whom death is preferable, are *not* morally justified in doing themselves a good turn, but must wait for someone else to do it for them.[7]

Bluck explains the meaning of this complicated passage as follows:

The surprizing fact is not the universal applicability of the doctrine that death is preferable to life, but the wickedness (in spite of that doctrine) of suicide . . . The soul, however much it may be tainted, stands a better chance of attaining some knowledge of truth, or at any rate of receiving desirable and needful conversion, when separated from the body. Teleologically speaking, the period of death is more valuable in many ways for everyone than the period of life (though the gods, we must suppose, know better than we do when is the appropriate time for us to die).[8]

Bluck has much Platonic exegesis on his side.[9]

After stating that the paradox appears irrational the second part of the argument begins. It inquires into the intelligibility of the traditional ban on suicide.

But perhaps it has something rational about it. Now the doctrine which is taught in secret about these matters, that we men are in a kind of prison and must not set ourselves free or run away seems to me to be very weighty and not easy to understand. But this at least appears to me to be correct that the gods are our guardians and that we men are one of the chattels of the gods.

What is the force of the "secret doctrine" that the body is the "prison" of the soul?

The first meaning of "prison" to be considered is that one is justly imprisoned in the body. If this is the case then one is "doing time" for some crime committed in a previous life. Wouldn't the complete acceptance of this interpretation make the ban on suicide intelligible, inasmuch as man must remain in prison until he has atoned for his crime? Let us follow the logic of this interpretation. One is imprisoned by higher authorities (the gods) and they determine the length of one's incarceration. Since one cannot escape from the judgment of the gods, escape from prison would not relieve one of his guilt but would only add to it. Much the same we would say that a criminal who escaped from prison before his sentence expired would be compounding his crime by his very escape, no matter how little time he had left to serve. One must wait until those who imprisoned him decree he is free of guilt and hence free to leave prison. This is certainly so where one does not even know the nature of his guilt. This might explain the paradox, does it not?

On the one hand, it would explain why death is better than life, for life is itself punishment for pre-natal sin, and one surely desires to be free of guilt and punishment. On the other hand, the only way one can escape from all this is through a complete atonement, and this he cannot do for himself. Only the gods could do it for him. Only they can bring atonement because, it is presumed, only they know the exact nature of the crime and the extent of its effects. Since the crime took place in a previous life of which one has no immediately conscious recollection, he himself is suffering the effects of an act whose cause is hidden from him. Therefore, he needs someone who has greater knowledge virtue and power than he, someone who can help him overcome this past guilt and finally be free of it. Only this greater person, or persons, can determine when the price has finally been paid. Here we see the Orphic doctrine as a clearly coherent explanation.[10] The gods, the guardians of the human person, finally relieve him of his embodied punishment for the primordial sin and help him once again return to the lost, pre-natal paradise.

However great the affinities between such an approach and the theory of recollection, it is inconsistent with the teaching of the *Phaedo*. The body is not regarded as a punishment, either just or unjust. The body is not keeping the soul from a state of blessedness on the "other side of the prison wall." For if such were indeed the case the body would be an insurmountable barrier to the soul's activity of philosophy, just as a prison wall is an insurmountable barrier to a prisoner's exercise of his freedom.

Through philosophy one is, in this life, already able to begin to overcome the impediment of the body as the organ of sense. Death is the final victory, but it is not the only victory. One is able to overcome the evils of embodiment one by one. One is not separated from vision of the forms because of something he did in a previous life of which he is now unaware and over which he has no control. One is separated from vision of the forms because of his own self-made condition in this life, and this alienated condition can be overcome by philosophy. Philosophy, although its dialectical beginning presupposes an outside interlocutor, is essentially the individual person's rational exercise of his own soul. Therefore, its function is within one's own rational grasp. (This is the very discovery which made Socrates turn away from Anaxagoras' theory of unconscious causes. It was ultimately anti-philosophical.[11]) If we followed the Orphic theory to its logical conclusion we would be forced to concede that death is the only freedom from the body.[12] By doing this, however, we would be destroying philosophy. Philosophy is essentially self-therapy, not salvation from someone wholly other.[13]

Nevertheless, there is a second sense of the term "prison" which might well avoid the pitfalls of just punishment, which would make the whole longing for death exclude philosophical experience. Couldn't we understand the meaning of "prison" as what we would today call *protective custody?*[14] I am not thinking so much of the type of protective custody in which a person is incarcerated because someone else is pursuing him, but rather the type of custody where a person is institutionalized because he is unable to care for himself.

Let us take the mentally ill as an example. Now in current psychiatric thinking institutionalization is not meant to be permanent, especially if the patient is young and not suffering organic brain damage. The institutionalization is to give the patient a protective environment *until* he is able to function on his own in the open world.[15] And the patient prepares for his eventual release from the mental hospital gradually, with the aid of a therapist, by overcoming the confines of his protective environment.

When he is first admitted he might be so disturbed that he needs to be confined in a padded seclusion room. Gradually he is able to function in a closely supervised ward situation, perhaps becoming coherent enough to begin self-examination in psychotherapy. After a while he might gain ground privileges, work privileges, live on an unlocked ward, return home for extended visits. The patient himself usually can understand when he is ready to leave the hospital, but the final decision is made by his therapist, and the final discharge is by authority of the hospital's superintendent, who authorized the initial hospitalization.

Many of course never reach this point and continue to regress. Nevertheless the very rationale of the hospital is that some can and will progress. On the one hand, unauthorized leave from the hospital indicates an avoidance of the fulfillment of therapy. It indicates an act of rebellion against the therapeutic process. On the other hand, the therapist must always reckon with the patient's resistance to being cured, which in this particular setting commonly called *institutionalism*. This indicates the patient's overdependence on the institutional confines and his refusal to strive towards freedom and full responsibility.

Because of this ever-present possibility, mental institutions cannot make themselves so securely inviting and conflict-free that the patient can draw the conclusion that this is exactly the place to find his life's fulfillment. Conversely, they cannot make themselves "snake-pits" where patients are punished for the "crimes" of the past, and where conditions which preclude any humane treatment for the patients further dehumanize them.

These institutions must be constructed paradoxically: they must be capable of providing protective therapy, but they must not be so protective so that their very environment suggests permanence to the patient. The patient must be stimulated to strive for release without escape. He must recognize his growing independence without losing sight of his dependence, which he only partially understands.

I believe this lengthy analogy explains what the *Phaedo* means when it refers to the body as being a *kind of prison,* but not prison in the usual sense. The soul needs the body in order to overcome it. Without the givenness of the body there would be no dialectic, no philosophy, which begins with the paradoxical data the body senses.[16] Nevertheless, the soul cannot settle permanently into the body. The body must be taken as unsettling and confusing.[17]

After Cebes agrees to the point about our being one of the chattels of the gods the argument continues.

If one of your slaves should kill himself when you had not indicated you wanted him to die, would you not be angry with him and
punish him if you had someone to punish? . . . Then perhaps on the
basis of this it would not be unreasonable that one must not kill himself but must wait until god sends some necessity, such as has now
come to me. (62C)

Here an analogy has been proposed with the ownership of slaves. The
notion he presents is that slaves are the absolute property of their masters
and they have no right to attempt escape from servitude, self-destruction
being the most radical way of escape. Thus any attempt to deprive the
master of his property, either by removing it from his domain, or by destroying the property itself, is unjust. Now what would be the motive
behind such attempts at deprivation? First, the motive might be to *gain
something of value from someone else.* Either A desires for himself B's
slave, C, or C desires for himself the freedom of his own person. Whether
the removal is caused by a third party (theft) or is self-caused by the slave
himself (escape), someone has taken something of value from the original
owner. A second motive might be destruction of the property itself,
namely, the motive is to *destroy something of value belonging to someone
else.* Either A desires to destroy B's property, his slave C, or C desires to
destroy himself thereby destroying B's property. In relation to the gods as
masters of man, then, what would be the motive of one who commits suicide? Is it to be free *from* the gods, or to deprive the gods of their
property?

Yet, whereas either motive or both motives might be explainable in
the case of human masters, neither of them is valid in the case of divine
masters, because the divine masters are assumed to be good, whereas
human masters may be evil. If a human master is evil, if he deprives his
slaves of what is to be theirs, then his slaves have some reason to attempt
escape *from* him or to do harm *to* him. However, the gods do not deprive
their human "chattels" of anything. Being good masters they have the
right to be angry with their chattels if they attempt either escape or destruction. The analogy between Cebes' situation as a human slave owner
and that of the gods is a fortiori in its logic: If you, a human slave owner,
being either good or not good, would be angry if one of your slaves attempted to escape or destroy himself, then may we not by right conclude
that the gods, who are surely good masters, would all the more so be angry
at suicide? They have done nothing to deserve such ingratitude.

Cebes tentatively agrees and then deepens the paradox.

> But what you just said, Socrates, that philosophers are to be
> ready and willing to die, that seems strange if what we just said is
> reasonable that god is our guardian and we are his chattels. For it is
> not reasonable that the most rational should not be angry when they
> leave the service in which the gods, *the best of overseers* are oversee-
> ing them . . . one possessing reason would always desire to be with
> him who is better than himself. And yet, Socrates, the contrary of
> what we just said seems to be so; for it seems that the rational are to
> be angry about dying, and the irrational are to rejoice. (62D-E)

Suicide is denied any rationale; servitude to the gods is good inasmuch
as the gods are good masters. If this is the case, then it would seem that
death, as the release from that very servitude, is not good, whether it is
self-caused (suicide) or caused by someone else. No rational being will be
happy over the loss of such a blessed condition. Whereas the emphasis on
the desirability of death for all seemingly made the ban on suicide irrational, here the emphasis on the blessed relationship with the gods on earth
seemingly makes the desirability of death irrational. It has still not been
shown how these two positions are reconcilable. Thus the paradox remains
in spite of the fact that both positions have been elaborated. Indeed this
very elaboration, now from one side now from the other, has deepened the
paradox.

At this point a conclusion is called for.

> For if I did not believe that I was going to other good and wise
> gods and, moreover, to men who have died, who are better than
> those here, I would be wrong not to fear death. Now you may be
> sure that I hope to go to good men, although I would not be abso-
> lutely certain of this, yet you may be sure that I am as certain of this
> as anything else concerning these matters, that I am going to gods
> who are good rulers. I not only do not grieve, but I am quite hopeful
> that there is something good for the dead, and as has been surely
> said of old, something better for the good than for the wicked.[24]
> (63B)

This concludes the "suicide text". And it is clear that the paradox
has been brought to a conclusion. After the elaboration of the two sides

of the paradox we are left with the following. One should desire death because freedom from the enclosure of the body finally enables the human soul to acquire pure knowledge. Identification with the body and its needs leads to confusion and ignorance.[18] The more one is able to separate from the body and its needs the more one is able to know the forms. When free from the body and capable of knowing the forms, the soul, which has "practiced dying", which has engaged in philosophy, "enters into the company (*genos*) of the gods",[19] and into the company of men "better than those here."

With this in mind we can see how the ban on suicide is consistent with the longing for death. One longs for death in order to see the forms. If he has "practiced dying" while his soul was yet in the body, he will reach this end and thereby be in the company of the gods. In other words, he will share something essential with the gods, he will participate in a *divine reality*. However, as is clear from many other passages, the gods precede humans in vision of the forms. Therefore, those persons who have truly prepared for death partake of the very divinity of the gods. Philosophy is a participation in divinity.

Life-after-death will not wholly surprise the prepared soul. The transition from life-before-death within the body to life-after-death without the body is not an absolute break, for philosophy has been able to connect the two realms. Two factors distinguish these two realms. First, before death knowledge of the forms is imperfect because the sense perceptions of the body can never fully be overcome while the soul is yet incarnate. Second, the relationship with the gods is different. In life-before-death we are the "chattels" of the gods; in life-after-death (if philosophically prepared) we are in the "company of the gods."

Now what essentially constitutes the distinction? We must consider that in this dialogue the relationship with the gods is twofold: on the one hand, they are causes who have power over us; on the other hand, they are living models of human life par excellence, namely, models of the philosophical life. As external causes we need only acknowledge that they are efficacious in human life. But as living models we must have some insight into their essence, because we must know *what* exactly admits us into their company, in what common reality we both participate. Now it is important to bear in mind that the transition from this world to the next is a transition from a relationship with the gods as causes to a relationship with the gods as associates. When this second relationship is characterized as "with other wise and good gods," it means an improved, a more mature relationship with the gods. One moves up from apprenticeship *under* the gods up to membership in their fraternity, or perhaps we might say into a "junior partnership" *with* them.

Why can humans not effect this transition when they believe themselves ready? The answer seems to be that the paradox that has been with us since the beginning of the "suicide text" has now become a paradoxical or ambivalent relationship with the gods. On the one hand, we are subservient to them as our masters; on the other hand, we are capable of eventual companionship with them in contemplation of the forms.

Both life and death involve a relationship with the gods. How can one ever be sure what his motives are in committing suicide? In one perspective it may be assumed that he is carrying out his insatiable desire to be with the gods as their companion in contemplation; but in another perspective he may be carrying out his contempt for the gods as they have made and preserved his body. Just as we discovered that the relationship with the body is ambivalent, so also is the relationship with the gods. As models of contemplation they beckon us to *come up with* them; as causes of incarnate life they bid one to *stay down under* them. In this life one can never be sure which aspect of divinity, is governing in any particular situation.

Suicide, although the self-caused termination of life, is still within life. Its only rational motive in this context could be that one believes himself ready and capable to end his incarnate apprenticeship to his divine masters. But how can man be sure that his apprenticeship is over? Rational suicide presupposes that the soul has perfect knowledge of its own state. Furthermore, rational suicide presupposes that one has perfect knowledge of his status in the life-after-death. Yet how can one be so sure of this when he has no conscious experience of life-after-death, but only a "good hope?"

One cannot positively act in such an enigmatic situation.[20] Thus suicide can only be explained in terms of this life. Here and now we can surely see it as an act of destruction of the property of the gods. It is an act of contempt for the divine masters. Such contempt can never lead to the desired companionship. Even if one is admitted to the companionship of the gods, he is still their junior in that he has sojourned within the body in the realm of becoming.

Compared to the gods man is always an *arriviste* in the realm of the forms. Suicide is an attempt to negate this past and a demand for instant equality. It is an attempt to erase the fact of the embodied state of dependence. But this is a denial of the truth; and how can one achieve the end of vision of Truth per se when his means of getting there have been rooted in a covering up of a major truth about man: the truth of his embodied dependence on the gods?

What the *Phaedo* seems to be saying is that the attempt to resolve this paradox by human means cannot achieve the end desired. Only the gods can resolve the paradox in that they alone have perfect knowledge of us. They alone have perfect knowledge of the realms of being and becoming. This is the force of Socrates' words, "until god sends some necessity upon him, such as now has come upon me." It is the gods who send necessity; man must do nothing but wait. On the one hand, he can escape the Athenian prison as Crito has urged him to do.[21] On the other hand he can attempt suicide, which is the attempt to escape the rule of the gods:

If he would opt for the first alternative, that is, escape from prison, he would be limiting the relationship with the gods to their role as masters of the embodied life; he would be resisting death. If he would opt for the second alternative, that is, suicide, then he would be limiting the relationship with the gods to their role as models of the disembodied life; he would be resisting life. However, Socrates does not know. He has experienced both aspects of divinity, both orders of the gods. Therefore, any action would assume knowledge which is not his. He can only hope for death, for hope can be based on belief.[22] But he cannot act for death, for action must be based on knowledge. All he can do is stand still and let god do whatever he decides. To do anything more than this passive acceptance would be a denial of the causality of the gods, something in which Socrates believes.[23]

Neither active alternative will resolve the paradox. Quite the contrary, either suicide or escape from prison will cover up some major truth. Only passive acceptance of the paradox makes its eventual solution an open possibility. Thus Socrates reiterates: "And while we live, we shall, I think, be *nearest to knowledge* when we avoid, *so far as possible,* intercourse and communion with the body, except what is absolutely necessary, and we are not filled with its nature, but keep ourselves pure *until god himself sets us free."* [24] [Italics mine.]

We have seen that Plato examines the question of suicide in terms of the inevitable life choice before Socrates in his final days. From careful analysis of the extremely cryptic language used there, we have seen that suicide was taken to be a problem arising from two human relationships: the relationship with the body, and the relationship with the gods. The essentially ambivalent character of both of these relationships prevents Socrates from choosing either to commit suicide or to escape from prison, for either active choice would be based on only one factor of the respective relationships at the expense of the other. However, philosophical examination has determined that no factor can be eliminated in truth. Therefore, Socrates has ruled out both active alternatives because of the equivocal nature of the relationship with the body which leads into the more fundamentally equivocal relationship with the gods. He is thus left with the passive alternative of waiting for God to act on his behalf. This then is the ethical conclusion of the "suicide text" in the *Phaedo*.

However, the *Phaedo* does not deal with the question of suicide in terms of the relationship with society. Of course in that particular context this is not a matter of ethical relevance for Socrates; his society, Athens, has already sentenced him to death. Furthermore, the means for that death sentence is for him to administer the death potion to himself.[25] This act is obviously taken to be of different ethical meaning than suicide.[26] It is not essentially self-caused, and intelligible self-causation is the criterion, first established in the *Phaedo* itself, for determining ethically relevant questions.[27] One is only responsible for acts resulting from his own rational decisions. The context of discussion always plays an important role in the structure of any of Plato's dialogues. In the *Phaedo* Socrates' relationship with society is already out of his hands. Hence, there, ethical concern with the social implications of suicide is precluded.

3. *Laws 873 C-D*.

The *Laws* 873 C-D contains Plato's later treatment of suicide. Here he deals with it in a social context in keeping with the subject matter of this dialogue. Nevertheless, this treatment does not confine itself to the social implications of suicide, but also attempts to comprehend suicide in terms of a man's relationship with his body and a man's relationship with the gods.

> Now he that slays the person who is, as men say, nearest and dearest of all, what penalty should he suffer? I mean the man that slays himself, violently robbing himself of his fate-given share of life, when this is not legally ordered by the State, and when he is not compelled to it by the occurence of some intolerable and inevitable misfortune, nor by falling into some disgrace that is beyond remedy or

endurance, but merely inflicting upon himself this iniquitous, penalty owing to sloth and unmanly cowardice. In this case, the rest of the matters concerning the rules about rites of purification and of burial come within the cognizance of the god, and regarding these the next of kin must seek information from the interpreters and the laws dealing with these matters, and act in accordance with their instructions; but for those thus destroyed the tombs shall be, first, in an isolated position without even one adjacent, and secondly, they shall be buried in those borders of the twelve districts which are barren and nameless, without note, and with neither headstone nor name to indicate the tombs.[28]

In this text Plato is dealing with three questions: (1) Which suicides may be judged by society and which may not? (2) In those suicides judged by society what traditional religious measures are to be taken? (3) In those suicides judged by society, what new measures are to be introduced in virtue of the nature of the crime of suicide?

In the *Phaedo* suicide seems to have been categorically declared immoral no matter what the circumstances. This has been noted by several scholars. "In the *Phaedo* (62a) it is suggested that suicide may be the only action which is always wrong. In the case of all other types of action it depends on the circumstances." [29] Here in the *Laws* we do have exceptions. How are we to understand the introduction of these exceptions? Did Plato's view change since the *Phaedo*? Now this is most plausible in that these respective prohibitions of suicide were written during different periods of Plato's life and the very words themselves are placed in the mouths of different men: in the *Phaedo* Socrates is speaking; in the *Laws* it is the Athenian stranger. However, in order for there to be a contradiction two mutually exclusive statements must be made about the same thing. In the *Phaedo* Plato is dealing with suicide as a dilemma for the philosopher (Socrates) in the antiphilosophical city of Athens. The individual significance of suicide is at issue. In the *Laws* Plato is dealing with public policy regarding the social significance of suicide for a society constructed according to philosophical ends.

The fact that only certain types of suicide are considered to be socially reprehensible does not automatically mean that Plato is condoning those other types of suicide which are not of social interest. The city, however, is only immediately concerned with those types of suicide which have direct bearing on the individual's relation to his community. Plato indicates that he is dealing with the type of suicide where the person is able to make a rational and deliberate decision. He rules out any compulsion, whether it be an external decree of the state, where the person is *given* suicide as the only alternative, or the internal compulsion of overwhelming emotions in the face of situations inevitable and beyond endurance. The city, based on reason, is made up of essentially rational components. Therefore, only the rational acts of rational persons are of direct concern. Empirically speaking, the city loses a citizen through a successful act of suicide irrespective of how or why the act was committed. If suicide is wrong it is clearly too late to punish the wrongdoer. Yet, rationally speaking, the motives for suicide are important to the city, because if suicide is an act rationally and deliberately chosen, without compulsion and with different options available, then the motive must be a free rejection by the person of his present milieu, the city. Suicide in this context becomes a fundamental rejection of the authority of the divinely oriented city.[30]

In cases of overwhelming misfortune the person is rejecting the accidental circumstances of his own particular situation. In this case, however, the person is rejecting his participation in the social whole, his very sociality. Irrational suicide is of no more concern than any other accidental death; it is not essentially a human rational option; it is the result of chance defects. However, rational suicide is of tremendous concern because it is the rejection of the authority of the city which is presented as the highest embodiment of reason available to man. Hence, in order to understand the social significance of suicide, the subject of this text in the *Laws*, we must understand wherein Plato places the source of the community's authority over the rational individual, and this individual's responsibility in the face of that authority.

When we see the social significance of suicide as part of this larger question of social responsibility we are able to locate in the *Republic* an important antecedent of this larger question.

Like other antecedents we will bring up, it requires detailed examination. However, this is necessary because the prohibition of suicide in the *Laws* is presented in statutory form. As such it presupposes an intricate process of philosophical development of more general principles from which the prohibition of suicide is concluded.

It has been assumed that the *Laws* is a further application of some of the principles of social philosophy first developed in the *Republic*.[31] The question of man's responsibility to the philosophically constituted city comes up in the *Republic* where the question is raised: Why should the philosopher, after having achieved the highest human goal, vision of the forms, be obligated to come down to the life of society again? Is this not contrary to the essential upward thrust which justifies the entire constitution of the *politeia*? Plato explains why the philosopher's responsibility to exercise enlightened leadership is indeed a just obligation for him. Three reasons are given.

> (1) Well then, if he recalled to mind his first habitation and what passed for wisdom there, and his fellow bondmen, do you not think that he would count himself happy in the change and pity them?[32]
>
> (2) Do you mean to say that we must do them this wrong, and compel them to live an inferior life when the better is in their power? . . . the law is not concerned with the special happiness of any class in the state, but is trying to produce this condition in the city as a whole . . . it itself creates such men in the state with a view to using them for the binding together of the commonwealth.[33]
>
> (3) You are the recipients of a more complete education than the others, and you are more capable of sharing both ways of life.[34]

The three reasons for social responsibility for the philosopher are logically connected.

The philosopher pities those who are left behind, those who are separated from his experience of enlightenment. Plato is not establishing "pity" here as a new virtue readymade for the occasion.[35] Indeed, pressing pity as a primary motive will get us nowhere. Rather, the pity of the philosopher is due to his philosophical experience of unity. The good to be sought is the one.[36] As such, his desire for the good involves a desire for the most complete possible participation in the philosophical enterprize. Everyone must be involved in the philosophical experience of unity to the best of his ability. This experience leads to a program of unification. For the ordinary, nonphilosophical citizen, this means being part of a society where philosophers are the leaders. The relationship of the philosopher to his fellow, nonphilosophical, citizens is not grounded in pity. Pity is the direct emotional response the philosopher must use in order to relate to those around him. Concern is a precondition for dialogue. Philosophers lead by gentle rational persuasion. This is the whole attraction of Socrates' personality.

Now if the philosopher willingly and actively remained aloof and in effect abandoned the city when he is needed the most for leadership; if he were to turn his back on his fellow citizens, unconcerned with their ultimate good, then he would be creating a fundamental schism in the life of society. His very experience of the good as unity ought to preclude such action, for how can an experience of the most fundamental ontological unity practically result in the most fundamental social schism? Surely Plato's social philosophy and ethics are rooted in his metaphysics. If the practical consequence of the ontological vision is such blatant alienation, then the very authenticity of the vision is seriously called into question. Philosophical irresponsibility would fragmentize the city. Even imperfect Athens is the object of the genuine and deep concern of Socrates.[37] Suicide would constitute a similar case of irresponsibility.

This striving for total participation is also necessary viewed from the negative side, lest antiphilosophical political forces arise within the city, creating a dichotomy between the soul of the philosopher and his bond with the political body. Such was the tragedy of the philosopher, Socrates, in the anti-philosophical city, Athens.

This political tragedy continually haunted Plato, as he warned:

> But the chief penalty is to be governed by someone worse if a man will not himself hold office and rule. It is from fear of this, as it appears to me, that the better sort hold office when they do, and then they go to it not in the expectation of enjoyment nor as to a good thing but as to a necessary evil, and because they are unable to turn it over to better men than themselves or to their like.[38]

This attitude is necessary for the sake of continuity. Philosophy is perpetuated by actual philosophers stimulating potential philosophers.[39] For the sake of the continued unity of philosophical experience the philosopher ought to perpetuate political and philosophical symbiosis. Plato refers to the philosopher as "the vigilant guardian of the polity."[40] Just as the city has its stake in the philosopher, the philosopher has his stake in the city. Suicide would have the same political consequences as the selfish refusal to assume civic responsibility.

Furthermore, because the philosopher always remains part of the realm of Becoming while still alive, his soul continues to be triparte even though intellectual self-mastery has been achieved.[41] His rational faculty (*nous*) still has need of the two lower faculties, the "spirited" and the "appetitive." Politically this means that the non-philosophers are neces-

sary for the philosopher. It is to be remembered that the three parts of the
ideal city are the exact macrocosm of the triparte soul.[42] As we determined
in the previous section, the soul has need of the body and its sensuous
"knowledge" until god reclaims it.

Finally, the philosopher is grateful to the city, but this gratitude is not
something externally imposed on him. If it were it would be neither just
nor successful. Plato insists on the justice of requiring the philosopher,
even after vision of the forms, to exercise social responsibility.

> . . . for we shall be imposing just commands on men who are just.
> Yet they will assuredly approach office as an unavoidable necessity,
> and in the opposite temper from that of the present rulers in our
> cities.[43]

The philosopher acts on internal motivations alone. Indeed the city can
hardly in justice coerce the philosopher to act against his own principles,
for the city itself is but the truly harmonious soul of man in macrocosm.[44]

The philosopher is grateful to the city, because the city has provided
him with the necessary means to reach his blessed state.[45] Now the city is
able to supply three things: physical necessities; social order; and philosophically oriented education.[46] Gratitude is in proportion to what the city
has actually done for the individual. In the famous passage in the *Crito*
(51E), where Socrates argues the case for obedience to the laws of Athens,
imagining an actual dialogue between himself and them, his point is that
his obedience is to be in direct proportion to that which he has received
from the city. Now Athens, or any ordinary city, provides physical necessities and social order, in this particular case the protection of law is emphasized. Since, however, Athens did not provide Socrates with his philosophical orientation, Athens is not deserving of his ultimate loyalty as a
philosopher.[47] Athens, then, fulfills the needs of the two lower faculties of
the soul, namely, the appetitive and the spirited. However, the Republic,
which fulfills the needs of the complete triparte soul, is obviously deserving
of the philosopher's ultimate loyalty. The Republic, like the later polity
envisioned in the *Laws,* is divine in intent and constitution.[48]

Only in the context of this kind of society can the social significance
of suicide, as an act of desertion, be adequately understood. Without the
background of the *Republic* the importance of the introduction of the
social factor of suicide in the *Laws,* in contradistinction to the *Phaedo*

where it is absent, could not be appreciated. As Plato's philosophy developed so did his treatment of specific problems, especially suicide.

It seems that there are three criteria for prohibiting suicide: namely, it ignores the importance of the body; it ignores the authority of the gods; and it ignores the philosopher's involvement in the philosophical city. We have seen that the first two criteria, namely the importance of the body and the importance of the gods, are related. How are the last two criteria, namely the importance of the gods and the importance of the city, related? In view of Plato's stout emphasis on seeing the unity behind seeming multiplicity, this is a very important question to ask if we are to fully understand his grounds for prohibiting suicide.

Obedience to the philosophical city and obedience to the gods are essentially the same. Both entities are "divine", that is, superior to man. Divinity (*to theion*) is an essence in which various divine beings participate. Divinity is predicable of its particulars; first and foremost the gods, but extending to other beings as well. This is at the very heart of Plato's polytheism.

> The Platonic teaching of a multiplicity of gods is puzzling, not to say forbidding to the casual reader . . . Plato rationalized Greek polytheism into the metaphysical doctrine of the One and the Many. The conception of the inferior gods with their specified regions of authority establishes the fact that the divine rule is particularized . . . The hierarchy of the gods is a particular application of the general principle of hierarchy which pervades all things . . . In order to be intelligible, an entity must be a structure, analyzable into elements in a relationship. The divine principle is a complex organic region of divine agencies in mutual interplay.[49]

In the *Phaedo* Plato can only speak of obedience to the gods as natural causes. He cannot, however, connect obedience to these natural causes with political obedience. For Socrates is an Athenian, and his status as a philosopher is in spite of Athens not because of her. When Plato spoke of occasional philosophers "growing up spontaneously from no volition of the government in the several states" (*Republic* 520B), he most certainly has Socrates making an implicit reference to himself. Therefore, Socrates owes Athens no gratitude for his becoming a philosopher. His only loyalty to Athens is for his birth and physical development and for the protection of Athenian laws and institutions. This is why he refuses

to defy Athenian jurisdiction by escaping from prison. His ultimate loyalty
is to God, however.

> Men of Athens, I respect and love you, but I shall obey the god
> rather than you, and while I live and am able to continue, I shall never
> give up philosophy or stop exhorting you and pointing out the truth
> to any one of you whom I may meet.[50]

However, in the philosophical city there is no such dichotomy; obedience
to society and obedience to the gods are one and the same. This essential
unity is brought out by the very prohibition of suicide in the *Laws*. "I
mean the man that slays himself, violently robbing himself of his *fate-given
share of life, when he is not legally ordered by the state.*" [51] The necessary
station assigned by the gods and that assigned by the State are identical.
That is why Plato, in the *Laws,* can speak of them in the very same sentence, something he obviously could not do in the *Phaedo.* Thus, in order
to see why the *Laws* can speak of suicide in a new perspective we must
remember that between the *Phaedo* and the *Laws* lies the *Republic.*[52]

It is only in the *Laws* that the prohibition of suicide can be seen in
terms of three relationships: with the self, with the gods, and with society.
Having reached this point in our investigation we must see how these three
relationships involve an identical approach on the part of the human
person. Inasmuch as the relationship with the body leads into the relationship with the gods, and the relationship with society is part of the relationship to the overall divine reality, we must further scrutinize the relationship with the gods in which the other two are ultimately grounded.
Examination of this relationship will show the development of Plato's
prohibition of suicide. The introduction of the social factor not only adds
something new, but it also indicates a new way of understanding the relationship with the gods, which is the basis of the prohibition both in the
Phaedo and in the *Laws.*

We have seen that the relationship with the body is dialectical. The
soul needs the body but must at the same time overcome it. The soul's
journey to vision of the forms involves a most intimate interaction with
the body. Platonic dualism is misunderstood when it is not viewed as a
dialectical relation between the body and the soul. Furthermore, the soul's
journey involves a dialectical relationship with society. The philosopher
working through his involvement with the city journeys towards that vision
which the city can point to but cannot itself provide. Human responsibility

becomes defined through this dialectic. The dialectic of the soul's relationship with the body leads into the relationship with the gods because the presence of the body calls for a causal explanation. This is most fully explicated in the creation myth in the *Timaeus*.[53]

The dialectic of the soul's relationship with the city also leads into the relationship with the gods because the founding of the philosophical city calls for a causal explanation. It is ultimately the gods who found the Republic. The ideal society cannot itself arise out of the grossly imperfect societies seen throughout human history. Plato is adamant on this point.

> Then the nature which we assumed in the philosopher, if it receives the proper teaching, must needs grow and attain to consummate excellence, but if it be sown and planted and grown in the wrong environment, the outcome will be quite the contrary, *unless some god comes to the rescue*.[54] [Italics mine.]

Plato makes the entire realization of the Republic contingent on the gods.

> . . . neither city nor polity nor man either will ever be perfected until some chance compels this uncorrupted remnant of philosophers, who now bear the stigma of uselessness, to take charge of the state whether they wish it or not, and constrains the citizens to obey them, or else *until by some divine inspiration a* genuine passion for true philosophy takes possession either of the sons of men now in power and sovereignty, or of themselves.[55] [Italics mine.]

At this point it seems that both the body and the city are the products of divine, that is, super-human, causality. The question now is: Is the divine causality of the philosophical city the same as the divine causality of the human body? If it is, then we now know of a new effect, but our knowledge of the cause remains the same. Thus we have a new application of the suicide prohibition, but the intelligibility of its ground remains unchanged. If, on the other hand, the consideration of the social factor in suicide is the result of understanding divine causality in a new way, then our knowledge of the ground of the prohibition has developed. Thus, we hope to see how Plato's view of human responsibility to the gods grew in the course of his philosophy, and with it his understanding of the prohibition of suicide.

Although there is a dialectic of the soul's relationship with the body there is no dialogue. The body and the soul obviously do not converse. Therefore, the body does not immediately participate with the soul in its rational discursive activity. The body is a problem which the soul must rationally overcome. This the soul does by inference. The problematic presence of the body is overcome by seeing it as the effect of the causality of the gods. As external causes, one need only acknowledge *that* the gods are somehow efficacious in human life. However, since the very object before us in the beginning is not a discursive entity, the cause explaining this object's facticity need not be considered as a discursive entity either. This is why, in terms of life as connection with the body, the human relationship with the gods is that of *chattel*. It is only after death, in this context anyway, that humans have anything in common with the gods.

The relationship with others in philosophical discourse is different. Unlike the relationship with the body, one converses with the object immediately present. The dialectic of social relations is initiated in dialogue. As such, the very nature of the data immediately present will require a different inquiry into the mode of its causality. How could society, which is essentially the communion of rational, discursive, persons, be established by anything less than a discursive being?

This causal precondition is brought out by examining the previously quoted passage from the *Republic*. There Plato speaks of divine causality twice.

(1) ". . . neither city nor man either will ever be perfected *until some chance compels* . . . and *constrains* citizens to obey . . ." This first reference refers to divine causality in the mode of external efficacy, namely, where the cause forces an effect on something less powerful whether they have something essentially in common or not. Here Plato is talking about the visible, physical aspects of the governing of the city, aspects which his practical political insight never allowed him to ignore or underestimate.

However, in his second reference to divine causality Plato is talking about something different. (2) ". . . or until *by some divine inspiration a genuine passion for true philosophy takes possession* . . ." Here he eliminates "necessity" and "chance" and speaks of something more personal, *someone* who instills philosophical eros.[56] Now how is this eros instilled? Here again one ought to look to the personality of the embodiment of the true philosopher, Socrates. Socrates instills the philosophical passion by engaging others in rational discourse. Philosophy can only be instilled philosophically. It should be noted once again that political behavior can be established by external compulsion, but a philosopher can only act philosophically on the basis of inner persuasion by reason.

Let us now examine how the relationship with the gods stimulates philosophy; and why suicide may be the most radical rejection of the philosophical enterprise. In dealing with the connection of the gods and philosophy Plato presents it on two levels: divine command and *imitatio Dei*.

In the earlier dialogues, especially in the *Apology,* the theme of direct divine inspiration, the *Daimon,* is explicated. The "god" or the "sign" is acknowledged to be the starting point for Socrates' activity as a philosopher.[57] Philosophy is the result of a commandment of the god.[58] Socrates acknowledges that he believes this commandment to be good, in keeping with the conclusion of the *Euthyphro* where the essence of Socrates' philosophical theology is established: namely, the gods love that which is right *per se,* what is right is not so because the gods happen to love it.[59] Therefore, the first point to be made is that philosophy is not good simply because the gods command it. The gods command it because it is good; hence man participates in the Good by his philosophical activity and obeys the god because the god had a greater and prior involvement in that which is good. The difference between Socrates and the god, inasmuch as they both participate in that which is good, is one of degree not of kind. The gods are better than Socrates, that is why it is "disgraceful to do wrong and to disobey him who is better than I, *be he god or man.*" Thus the judgments of "good" and "better" are meaningless lest they be grounded in what is good per se.

If so, then why the divine imperative at all? This question is crucial for the suicide prohibition. Actually, this question, although never raised in the *Euthyphro,* is certainly implied in its conclusion. An answer to this crucial question has been attempted by subsequent exegetes.[60] If the gods are no longer considered as first principles, wherein lies their superiority, wherein lies man's obligation to obey them? This question underlies the prohibition of suicide in both the *Phaedo* and the *Laws.*

In order to understand this human responsibility we must remember that man approaches the vision of the forms dialectically, that he must patiently work his way through opposing options on ever deeper levels. And Platonic dialectic is always the result of dialogue. There is no dialectic without direct person-to-person discourse. The dialogical precondition ought to be kept in mind by modern students whose associations with the term "dialectic" are almost automatically colored by its meaning in the Hegelian tradition.[61]

That dialectic is the result of dialogue can be seen in Plato's treatment of self-knowledge. Socrates speaks of self-knowledge, or self-examination, when he alludes to the command of the god "to spend my life in philosophy and in examining myself and others." Of course his most famous statement about self-knowledge is his approval of the ancient philosophers of Crete and Sparta, and especially of their well-known maxim, "Know Thyself." [62] Nevertheless, just what sort of self-knowledge is possible? Plato eliminates a simple self-knowledge, where the self is simultaneously subject and object, by the law of noncontradiction.[63]

This application of the law had tremendous influence. Philo summarized it and presented an excellent analogy in the similar inability of the eye to see itself.[64] Plotinus went so far as to deny the very words used by Socrates "know thyself" (gnothi sauton), inasmuch as knowledge presupposes a bifurcation of the knowing subject from the known object which is impossible when they are identical.[65]

Therefore, the only way to understand self-knowledge is in the context of dialogue. Examination of one's self is only possible in the dialogical act of examining others. Only in discourse is one able to see the content of his opinions and whether they stand up to critical examination or not. Self-knowledge is only a possibility when pursued through the eyes of an outside interlocutor. Self and others are the objects of the same act of examination.[66]

Since all of philosophy is the examination of one's own opinions, it would seem to follow that philosophizing is impossible without dialogue. As such the very inception of philosophy presupposes an outside interlocutor, one who has already seen the forms, vision of which is the goal of all philosophy.[67] Without this priority dialogue would be a case of "the blind leading the blind." Who then is the original interlocutor and how does he function?

At this point we must return to the *Apology*.

"... something divine and spiritual comes to me ... I have had this from my childhood; it is a sort of a voice that comes to me, and when it comes it always holds me back from what I am thinking of doing, but never urges me forward." [68]

Socrates claims his experience to be original.[69]

God, then, causes Socrates to be a philosopher in two ways: He holds before him the generally irresistible urge to examine the opinions of himself and other men. He acts as a check on any particular rash or unexamined act Socrates might be contemplating. Socrates alludes to this constraining influence in crucial situations where important decisions are demanded.[70]

If we examine how Socrates himself functions as an interlocutor in dialogue with others we can see that he reflects what, by his own testimony, the god did with him. In the closely related dialogue, the *Crito,* Socrates becomes Crito's interlocutor concerning Crito's opinion that Socrates ought to escape from prison so as to avoid the death sentence of the Athenian court. There Socrates says to Crito: "So we must examine the question whether we ought to do this or not; for I am not now but always a man who follows nothing but the reasoning which on consideration seems to be best." [71]

When we compare this *Crito* passage with the *Apology* passage it is apparent that we are in essence hearing the same thing. The only restraint a philosopher can freely accept is the restraint of reason. The god seems to be the first person in the chain of dialogue. He might be referred to as the discursive presupposition.[72] Although Socrates is vague on this point, it would seem that the general urging and the particular restraint exercised by the god are expressed in rational discourse with him.

The *Daimon* spoken of in the *Apology* and the philosophical *eros* spoken of in the *Republic* are identified one with another in the Symposium by *Socrates'* teacher, the prophetess, Diotima.[73] The *Daimon,* then, is the philosophical manifestation of the gods. The somewhat vague *dialektos* of Diotima is developed by Plato into the uniquely philosophical *dialektike.* The philosophical city establishes the god's dialektos, which had heretofore been with individual men in isolated situations, into an organized program leading to enlightenment based on intelligent and patient social organization. Moreover, dialectic is seen both from within and from without as restraint. Negatively, the restraining character of dialectic is brought out by opponents to show that it might be an elaborate game of elimination having no necessary connection with truth.[74] Positively, it is simply presented as the characteristic of dialectic.[75]

My contention is that the Divine command Plato presents Socrates as respecting is in effect rational persuasion through dialogue. I am trying to show that the god is at the very inception of philosophy among humans, and that the relationship with the gods is crucial for both individual and social ethics, namely, ethics involving the relationship with oneself and ethics involving the relationship with society. Suicide, being a problem both for individual and social ethics, involves a relationship with the gods on both levels. We have already examined the relationship on the causal level. We must now clarify what is the relationship with the gods on the social level. This will show us that the prohibition of suicide on the basis of the social relationship will be different from the prohibition based on the individual, causal, level. It will be different in the sense of a deeper development not a contradiction. Moreover, the theme of *imitatio Dei,* which Plato begins to develop in the middle dialogues, makes this transition explicit.

The notion of *imitatio Dei* presupposes that *what* one has in common with the gods must be known in order for there to be this type of relationship between them. Being a relationship which one chooses, rather than one he already finds himself part of as a datum, as is the case in his status as "chattel" of the gods, *imitatio Dei* is a relationship initiated and nurtured by intelligent striving. It is a relationship with the gods involving philosophy. Philosophy is that which is between humans and the gods. The gods are the model for philosophical activity. Despite great distinctions in degree they are essentially the same in kind. They share a definable fellowship; they face common problems.

God is the first and foremost member in the order of "souls",[76] namely, individual centers of consciousness which perceive the forms. In the *Laws* God is specifically referred to as the "best soul." [77] And because the gods are in the order of souls, they have something essential in common with man who is also a "soul".[78] Inasmuch as the god is more of a soul than man, the god is the model for true humanization, or perhaps "divinization," of himself through the activity of philosophy. The god fulfills two criteria necessary for there to be an exemplary relationship: (1) the model must have something essential in common with whatever is to imitate it, for if not it would be remote beyond approach; (2) the model must stand in a relation of superiority to whatever imitates it inasmuch as a model beckons its imitator to rise up to its own level. If they were on an equal level the model would be too near to be a goal.[79] Plato urges one to move up to the level of the gods.[80] And we see that the approach to the gods is not direct, but rather, dialectical in that one must *work through* the presence of physical necessity. Despite the fact that both man and gods are souls, the human person must struggle through adversity to actualize his relationship with them. This is explained by the following comment:

The imitator of God, however, just because he is not God but man, has a *growth* in sameness. Since he never completely arrives, but only progressively approximates the goodness that is in God, his character pattern remains constant while he adapts himself more and more to it . . . Hence the imitator of God will be constantly examining himself in the light of the character of God, and seeking to do God's will better . . .[81]

Once we have established the essence of this linear relationship between humans and the gods, we can infer that human life is to be, ideally, on the basis of the divine model already present. Philosophy then becomes that *imitatio Dei* which a human is capable of by nature. The model not only indicates the status which is the aspiration of the philosophical life, but the *modus operendi* of that life as well.[82]

The gods as models for human philosophical activity are different than the forms. Both humans and the gods are ultimately beneath the forms. Therefore, despite their differences, both are faced with the problem of responsibility. Since both are *below* the forms and *above* the physical world, the problem is twofold: (1) both are *under* the forms; (2) both have responsibility *for* the world in their care. Thus the problem of re-sponsibility *for* the world is both human and divine. Since the gods pre-cede us in philosophy (that is why they are models), we ought to look and see how Plato describes the way they handled the problem of responsi-bility. We might ask: Do the gods face the problem of responsibility in the same way humans face it, especially as they do in the act of suicide?

We see the problem treated in the *Timaeus,* which many scholars regard as pivotal in the development of Plato's thought because they con-sider it to be the sequel to the *Republic* and the introduction to the later dialogues.[83] The problem of the creation (not *ex nihilo* of course) of the manifold, phenomenal world-order (cosmos), which Plato presents in an ontological context, is in truth an ethical problem.

Let us now state the cause wherefore He that constructed Becoming and the all. He was good, and in him that is good no envy ariseth ever concerning anything; and being devoid of envy He desired that all should be so far as possible, like unto Himself . . . this cosmos has verily come into existence as a living Creature endowed with soul and reason owing to the providence of God.[84]

The obvious question here is: Why does God who has perfect vision of the Forms concern himself with the imperfect realm beneath himself? Plato attempts to solve the paradox by introducing the notion of "envy" (*phthonos*) To ignore the world of becoming ill behooves a being which is good inasmuch as the only motive for this would be envy, which is inconsistent with goodness. However, the circular reasoning here is quite evident. If the "good" is the final end,[85] the movement towards which is a perfecting activity, then how can an already perfect being direct its concern towards objects whose condition is alien to that end? The attainment of that end involves flight from the world.[86]

Clearly, we cannot press the meaning of envy too deeply in our attempt to solve this problem.[95] However, it ought to occur to us here that the *moral* logic of this argument is the same as the first of Plato's arguments as to why the philosopher must return to the city to exercise his social responsibility even after he has participated in the vision of the forms (*Republic* 516C). There Plato puts forth "pity" (*eleos*) as the positive motive to be encouraged. Here he puts forth "envy" as the negative motive to be discouraged.[88]

_ *Pity* behooves the philosopher in his dealings with society. Envy ill behooves the god in his dealings with the world. Just as we discovered that pressing "envy" in and of itself for meaning does not fully satisfy us in this situation, so we discovered earlier that "pity" is not an adequate word to express the issue. What is at issue in both cases, however, is the question of unity.

One cannot attempt to totally transcend the earthly city nor can the god attempt to totally transcend the physical world, without each affecting a fundamental diremption in his own specific sphere of operation: humans in the social order; the god in the ontological order. Responsibility is demanded of both humans and gods. Neither one can turn his back on that which lies below him, for man is not the *creator ex nihilo* of his society and the god is not *creator ex nihilo* of the cosmos. Both must shape something already there. Both must act on behalf of the Good which alone is truly one.[89] Pity affects unity by drawing others near; jeolousy affects diremption because it separates one from others. Pity acts in the interest of the ultimate value; it is fundamentally responsible. Envy works against it; it is fundamentally irresponsible. That is why the former is good for both the gods and humans; the latter is bad for both. This problem of the god can now be seen as the model for human responsibility. The initiation of contact between humans and the gods comes from the gods themselves,[90] because they have already solved the problems which man is still facing.

Only when *imitatio Dei* is seen both from the side of man and from the side of the gods is it truly intelligible. Without understanding the passage from the *Timaeus* as ethical in meaning our knowledge of *imitatio dei* as the *modus operendi* of Platonic ethics is incomplete. One can imitate the gods and the gods can be imitated because the most fundamental ethical problem of responsibility is a problem for both: for the gods on the cosmic scale, for humans on the social scale. Suicide is an example of the larger question of responsibility, and as such it reflects a problem both human and divine.

4. *Conclusion*

We have seen that the social dimension of suicide can only be an integral factor in the rational prohibition of suicide in a society itself philosophically constructed. In the city of Athens, for example, responsibility *to* the god for the body, not responsibility *to* the actual society, prevents Socrates from making the rational choice to commit suicide.

However, it was also shown that the relationship with the god becomes more deeply understood when we see human sociality in philosophical perspective. For here the gods are seen not only as external causes of the union of body and soul which is the individual person, but as the discursive cause of the authentically human city as well. Moreover, seeing the intimate connection between dialectic and dialogue, we have discovered how, for Plato, an original interlocutor was necessary to initiate the dialogue rational human beings need to found a society worthy of their true nature. This necessity became more apparent when it was shown that self-knowledge can only be understood in the context of dialogue.

And finally, we have seen that this fundamentally rational and discursive relationship with the gods, expressed in Plato's conception of *imitatio Dei,* is the foundation of responsibility in Platonic ethics. Whereas in the *Phaedo* one is responsible *to* the gods, by the time of the *Laws,* and all the philosophical development underlying it, both humans *and* the gods are responsible *for* the respective worlds in their care. Thus it is in the context of a rational society that the relationship with the body beneath him and the gods above him is explicated and given deeper meaning.

The dialogical nature of the rational society integrates the three dimensions of suicide, namely, the relationship with the self as a body, the relationship with other rational human beings, and the relationship with the gods. Perhaps the fact that Plato condemns suicide as he does no other human action can now at last be understood. Suicide is the most disruptive of all human relationships. No other human action, no matter how wicked we believe it to be, is so comprehensively evil. For Plato, one is always involved in relations. Each of the three parts of the soul, which at superficial reading of Plato's description of them seem to be self-contained entities, each one of them can only be properly understood in relation to its respective object. The rational soul is related to the world of the forms which lie outside the soul itself.[91] The appetitive soul is related to the physical world outside itself. As for the spirited soul it is ambivalent: either it is related to the forms by being the enlightened servant of the rational soul, or it is related to the physical world by being the blind slave of the appetitive passions.

Dialogue is human sociality in deepest perspective, for it involves the relationship with the body, it flourishes and develops in relationship with other rational persons, and it is grounded in the relationship with the gods. The reflective Greek phrase used to designate suicide indicates that it is a self-passion. As such suicide rules out rational reflection which intends an external object. If the end of human life is *reflective* vision of the forms, then suicide cannot be the means whereby to accomplish this. The forms can only be reached by *imitatio Dei* which itself precludes suicide because suicide is fundamentally irresponsible, and the gods (in Plato's reconstruction of Greek theology) are models of responsible action. This is saying a good deal more than the earlier condemnation of suicide on the grounds that it is an arrogant rejection of our subordinate relationship to the gods. Furthermore, being the ultimate act of solitude, it permanently destroys the relationship with society, thus removing one from the arena of dialogue. Suicide being egocentricity in its most radical manifestation is the death of dialogue, the indispensible condition of philosophy. Nothing could be more immoral for Plato.

NOTES

1 H. M. Wolff, *Plato: Der Kampf ums Sein* (Bern: Francke Verlag, 1951), pp. 121-122.

2 Paul Friedländer, *Platon* III (Berlin: Walter de Gruyter, 1960), p. 35.

3 See *Enneads* I, 19.6; and *De Civitate Dei* I, 22.

4 "And rationality—that which is commonly called self-restraint, which consists in not being excited by the passions and in being superior to them and acting in a seemly way, is not that characteristic of those alone who make little of the body and spend their lives in philosophy?" *Phaedo,* 68C.

5 See R. Hackforth, *Plato's Phaedo,* (Cambridge: Cambridge University Press, 1955), p. 35, n. 1.

6 *Plato's Phaedo,* (Indianapolis and New York: Bobbs-Merrill, 1955), pp. 43-44.

7 Greek text ed. H. N. Fowler, Loeb Classical Library (Cambridge, Mass.: Harvard University Press, 1914). All Greek quotes from the *Phaedo* are taken from this edition.

8 Bluck, *Plato's Phaedo,* pp. 152-153.

9 Leonardo Táran, "Plato, Phaedo 62A", "*American Journal of Philology,* Vol. 87 (July, 1966), p. 326. In this article Taran analyzes and fully documents all of the opposing theories for the translation of this difficult passage. For varying translations and interpretations see, Hackforth, *Plato's Phaedo,* p. 191; Bluck, *Plato's Phaedo,* p. 151; Archer-Hind, *Phaedo* (New York: Macmillan, 1894), pp. 16-17; Fowler, Loeb ed., p. 215.

10 See A. E. Taylor, *Plato: The Man and His Work* (Edinburgh: Morrison and Gibb, 1927), pp. 178-179, E. Frank, *Plato und die Sogenannten Pythägorer* (Halle: Niemayer, 1923), pp. 293 ff.

11 Note: "My glorious hope, my friend, was quickly snatched away from me. As I went on with my reading I saw that the man made no use of intelligence and did not assign any real causes for the ordering of things, but mentioned as causes air and ether and water and many other absurdities." *Phaedo* 98C.

12 However, the *Phaedo* specifically indicates that philosophy is here and now. ". . . the true philosophers practice dying . . ." *Phaedo* 67E. The verb is in the present tense. Note also the lines above: ". . . it would be absurd if a man preparing himself *throughout his life* to live as close as possible to dying should then be disturbed when death *finally came."*

13 See John Wild, *Plato's Theory of Man* (Cambridge, Mass.: Harvard University Press, 1946), pp. 141-142.

14 Friedländer, *Platon,* III, p. 436, n.7.

15 For a classical treatment of the entire subject see William Alanson White, *Forty Years of Psychiatry* (Washington and New York: Nervous and Mental Diseases Publishing Co., 1933). I have constructed this analogy on the basis of my three years experience as chaplain at St. Elizabeth's Hospital in Washington, D. C.

16 See *Rep.* 523 ff.

17 See *Cratylus* 400C for Plato's distinction between "prison" as he uses it figuratively (*phroura*) and "prison" as the orphics more literally used it (*desmoterion*).

[18] "For the body keeps us constantly busy by reason of its need of nourishment; and moreover, if diseases come upon it they hinder our pursuit of the truth . . . it makes it truly impossible to reason altogether." *Phaedo* 66C.

[19] *Phaedo* 82C.

[20] Socrates' restraining words to Euthyphro should be recalled. "By Zeus, Euthyphro, do you think your knowledge about divine laws and holiness and unholiness is so exact that when the facts are as you say, you are not afraid of *doing something* unholy yourself in prosecuting your own father?" *Euthyphro* 4E [My trans.] Restraint is always advised when one does not possess firm knowledge; see *Protagoras* 312C, and *Menexenus* 234B.

[21] See *Crito* 44C ff.

[22] "These beliefs will gain in definiteness as we proceed; but it is well to realize now that for the Platonic Socrates, and for Plato himself, the *manner* of the soul's discarnate existence is always a matter of faith, not of knowledge, and one for the most part dealt with in myth." Hackforth, *Plato's Phaedo*, p. 42.

[23] ". . . the gods who are, *as you yourself agree* our masters." *Phaedo* 67C.

[24] *Phaedo* 67C.

[25] Note: "The boy went out . . . then came back with the man who was to give the poison, which he brought in a cup already prepared. When Socrates saw the man he said: "Well, my good fellow, you know about these things; *what am I to do?*' 'Nothing but drink it . . .'" *Phaedo* 117A.

[26] See *Crito* 50A ff.

[27] See Phaedo 97B ff. Cf. Aristotle, *Nicomachean Ethics* 1113b ff.

[28] *Laws* 873C-D, trans. R. G. Bury, Vol. I, Loeb Classical Library (Cambridge, Mass.: Harvard University Press, 1926), pp. 264-267.

[29] I. M. Crombie, *An Examination of Plato's Doctrines* I (London: Routledge and Kegan Paul, 1962), p. 254, n. 1. Note also: "Dass der Selbstmord, den der Platon unbedingt verwarf . . ." Ulrich von Wilamowitz—Moellendorf, *Platon* I, (Berlin: Weidmann, 1929); p. 697, n. 1.

[30] See *Laws* 716A ff.

[31] See R. S. Bluck, *Plato's Life and Thought* (London: Routledge and Kegan Paul, 1949), p. 143. Cf. Aristotle, *Politics* 1264b27 ff.

. [32] *Republic* 516C, trans. Paul Shorey, Vol. II, Loeb Classical Library (Cambridge, Mass.: Harvard University Press, 1937), pp. 126-127.

[33] *Rep.* 519D-520A.

[34] *Ibid.*, 520B-C.

[35] Nietzsche was right, I believe, about this when he wrote: "Diese moderne Philosophen Bevorzugung und Uberschätzung des Mitleidens ist nämlich etwas neues: gerade über den *Unwert* des Mitleidens waren bisher die Philosophen übereingekommen. Ich nenne nur Plato, Spinoza, Larochefoucald und Kant, vier Geister so verschieden voneinander als möglich, aber in einem eins: in der Geringschätzung des Mitleidens." *Zur Genealogie der Moral*, (Munich: Carl Hanser Verlag, 1967), p. 180.

[36] See *Rep.* 381B ff. Also regarding the unity of the city see *Rep.* 423D.

[37] See *Apology* 29D ff.

[38] *Rep.* 347C.

[39] ". . . when the turn comes for each toiling in the service of the state and holding office for the city's sake, regarding the task not as, a fine thing but as a necessity; and so, when each generation has educated others like themselves to take their place as guardians of the state . . ." *Rep.* 540B.

[40] *Rep.* 525B.

41 See *Rep.* 431A and 443D.

42 See *Rep.* 441A.

43 *Rep.* 520D. "The good and the necessary is a favourite Platonic antithesis, but the necessary is often the *conditio sine qua non* of the good." Paul Shorey, Loeb ed., vol. I, p. 80, n. b. For the futility of intellectual constraint see 536E.

44 "The ruling principle and its two subjects are at one in the belief that the reason ought to rule ... The virtue of rationality certainly ... is nothing else than this, whether in a city or an individual." *Rep.* 520B.

45 See *Rep.* 520B.

46 The education given by Athens is not philosophical. "Did those of us who are assigned to these matters not give good directions when we told your father *to educate you in music and gymnastics?*" *Crito* 50D, Loeb, ed., pp. 176-177.

47 "In a passage of Plato's *Crito,* Socrates is presented as deriving his duty of obedience to the city of Athens and her laws from a tacit contract. To understand this passage, one has to compare it with its parallel in the *Republic.* In the *Republic* the philosopher's duty of obedience is not derived from any contract. The reason is obvious. The city of the Republic is the best city, the city according to nature. But the city of Athens, that democracy, was from Plato's point of view a most imperfect city. Only the allegiance to an inferior community can be derivative from contract..." Leo Strauss, *Natural Right and History* (Chicago, Illinois: University of Chicago Press, 1953), p. 119.

48 "But if it ever finds the best polity as it itself is the best, then will it be apparent that this was in truth divine and all others human in their natures and practices." *Rep.* 497C. Cf. *Laws* 631B-D as to the distinction between goods human and goods divine. Also see J. B. Skemp, *The Theory of Motion in Plato's Later Dialogues* (Cambridge: Cambridge University Press, 1942), p. 109.

49 Raphael Demos, *The Philosophy of Plato* (New York: Chas. Scribner's Sons, 1939), pp. 113-114. See Taylor, *Plato,* p. 492, and Crombie, *An Examination of Plato's Doctrines* I, p. 371.

50 *Apology* 29D, Loeb ed., pp. 108-109.

51 *Moira* is divine action seen as the cause of necessary and inavoidable human states of affairs. "Destiny is personified as at *Phaedo* 115a." E. B. England, *The Laws of Plato* I (Manchester: Manchester University Press, 1921), p. 425. See *Laws* 960C-D.

52 For the scholarly opinion that the *Republic* follows the *Phaedo* in sequence, see Paul Shorey, Loeb ed., vol. II, p. 480; F. M. Cornford, *The Republic of Plato* (New York: Oxford University Press, 1945), pp. 341-345.

53 41C ff.

54 *Rep.* 492A; cf., *ibid.,* 493A.

55 *Rep.* 499B.

56 See Y. R. Simon, *Philosophy of Democratic Government* (Chicago: University of Chicago Press, 1951), p. 109 for an analysis of the difference between coercion and persuasion.

57 See *Apology* 23B. cf. "... the god gave me a station, as I believed and understood, with orders to spend my life in philosophy and in examining others ... But I know that it is evil and disgraceful to do wrong and to disobey him who is better than I, be he god or man." *Apology* 28E, 29B.

58 "For know that the god commands me to do this, and I believe that no greater good ever came to pass in the city than my service to the god." *Apology* 30A.

59 See *Euthyphro* 10A-E.

60 Note: "... the dilemma presented in the sceptical philosophy of Sextus Empiricus: 'Again, if the divine exists, either it has virtue or it has not. If it has not, then the divine is a poor and wretched thing, an absurd conclusion. If it has, then there will be something greater, or higher, than God; . . . But if it is greater, or higher, than God, evidently God, as deficient in nature, will be a poor thing and subject to corruption. But if there is no middle term between these opposites, and God cannot be seen to fall under either of them, then we must say that God is not.' (*Adv. Physicos* i, 176). P. E. More, *The Religion of Plato* (Princeton: Princeton University Press, 1921), pp. 39-40. Also see G. E. Mueller: "Plato and the Gods," *Philosophical Review* 45 (Summer, 1936), p. 461.

61 See Paul Shorey, *The Republic*, Loeb ed. Vol. II, p. 201, note f.

62 *Protagoras* 343B.

63 "Now the phrase 'master of himself' is an absurdity is it not? For he who is master of himself would also be subject to himself, and he who is subject to himself would be master. For the same person is spoken of in all these expressions." *Rep.* 431A.

64 See *Legum Allegoria* I, 39.91.

65 See *Enneads* VI, 7.15. For the first statement of the principle of non-contradiction in the very context of self-knowledge, see *Rep.* 436C and the note of Shorey, Loeb ed., Vol. I, p. 382, note a *ad locum*.

66 See *Apology* 28E.

67 See *Rep.* 540A.

68 *Apology* 31D.

69 See *Rep.* 496C. There is the Loeb ed. (Vol. II, pp. 52-53), Shorey notes: "The enormous fanciful literature on the daimonion does not concern the interpretation of Plato, who consistently treats it as a kind of spiritual tack checking Socrates from any act opposed to his true moral and intellectual interests." Also see J. van Camp and Paul Canart, *Le Sens du Mot Theios Chez Platon* (Louvain, 1956), p. 28.

70 "This which has happened to me is doubtless a good thing, and those of us who think death is an evil must be mistaken. A convincing proof of this has been given me; for the accustomed sign would surely have opposed me if I had not been going to meet with something good." *Apology* 40B-C, Cf. *Ibid.*, 41D.

71 *Crito* 46B, Loeb ed., pp. 160-161.

72 Note: "Imitation of God has special significance for human beings. Human beings are moral creatures whose possession of *nous* makes it possible for them consciously to achieve true manhood. In the effort to do this, they are portrayed in the dialogues as looking to the forms of justice, wisdom, temperance and the like. God as the 'ensoulment' of all these virtues becomes man's larger self (cf. *Pol.* 303b). As such he serves as a definite, individual example of imitation." C. G. Rutenber, *The Doctrine of the Imitation of God in Plato*, (New York: King's Crown Press, 1946), p. 38.

73 See *Symposium* 202E; also *Philebus* 16C; cf. 25B, 61C. Note also: "It might even be said that the 'daemonic' is the nearest equivalent in the Greek language for our word 'religion'. So Hug in his excellent note to the *Symposium* 202E: 'Den Damonen wird in diesen Satzen das ganze Gebiet der Religion zugewiesen, wofür den Griechen ein zusammenfassender Begriff fehlt.' " More, *The Religion of Plato*, p. 313, n. 15.

74 Note: "... just as by expert draught-players the unskilled are finally shut in and cannot make a move, so they are finally blocked and have their mouths stopped by this other game of draughts played not with counters but with words; yet the truth is not affected by that outcome." *Rep.* 487C; Cf. Aristotle, *Metaphysics* 1004b20 f.

75 See *Sophist* 253D; *Laws* 903A.

76 "Such is the life of the gods, but of the other souls, that which is best follows after God and is most like him . . ." *Phaedrus* 248A, Loeb, ed., pp. 476-477. See Taylor, *Plato*, p. 492.

77 *Laws* 897C.

78 Note: ". . . the fact that you believe in gods is due probably to *a divine kinship drawing you of what is of like nature* to honour it and recognize its existence." *Laws* 899D.

79 See Rutenber, *The Doctrine of the Imitation of God in Plato*, p. 37.

80 "Wherefore one ought to distinguish two kinds of causes, the necessary and the divine, in all things to seek after the divine for the sake of going to a life of blessedness, . . . and to seek the necessary for the sake of the divine, reckoning that without the former it is impossible to discern by themselves along the divine objects after which we strive, . . ." *Timaeus* 68E-69A, Loeb ed., pp. 176-179. Cf. *Phaedrus* 252E.

81 Rutenber, *The Doctrine of the Imitation of God in Plato*, p. 69. Note also: "God leads us towards the good life but the Good is not God. The Ideas constitute a second natural order, not a supernatural order. The Ideas are not personalities and the highest Idea is therefore not God." J. K. Feibleman, *Religious Platonism*, (London: Allen and Unwin, 1959), p. 75.

82 ". . . to escape is to become like God, so far as this is possible; and to become like God is to become righteous and holy and wise." *Theaetetus* 176 A-B, Loeb ed., pp. 127-130. Cf. *Rep.* 501B; *Philebus* 63E; *Laws* 716C.

83 "Looking deeper, we see that the chief purpose of the cosmological introduction is to link the morality externalised in the ideal society to the whole organization of the world. The *Republic* had dwelt on the structural analogy between the state and the individual soul. Now Plato intends to base his conception of human life, both for the individual and for society, on the inexpugnable foundation of the order of the universe." F. M. Cornford, *Plato's Cosmology*, (London: Routledge and Kegan Paul, 1937), p. 6.

84 *Timaeus* 29E-30C.

85 See F. Solmsen, *Plato's Theology* (Ithaca: Cornell University Press, 1942), p. 73.

86 *Theaetetus* 176B.

87 A. O. Lovejoy, who considers the text from the *Timaeus* to be one of the most seminal passages in the history of western philosophy, takes the whole description there to be a metaphor for a purely ontological problem. See *The Great Chain of Being*, (New York: Harper Torchbooks, 1962), pp. 48-49 Cf. Solmsen, *op. cit.*, pp. 151-152; Demos, *op. cit.*, pp. 104-105.

88 Cf. Aristotle, *Metaphysics* 982b-983a.

89 Note: "Like God in the cosmos, man in making a cosmos out of his own inner life takes what is already present and brings it to maximum order and value, eliminating only in extreme cases. Thus he will not despise the body in the interest of an extreme spirituality, but rather will use both the body and the goods of the body for the promotion of the total good of his life . . ." Rutenber, *The Doctrine of the Imitation of God in Plato*, p. 71.

90 See Rutenber, *op. cit.*, pp. 81, 97-98.

91 Note: "Knowledge, by definition, is of unique, unchanging objects . . . The Forms, however, are not laws of the sequence or coexistence of phenomena, but are ideals or patterns, which have a real existence independent of our minds. (Hence most modern critics avoid the term 'Idea', though this is Plato's word, because it now suggests a thought existing 'only in our mind.') . . ." Cornford, *The Republic of Plato*, p. 180.

CHAPTER III

SUICIDE AND HUMAN NATURE IN AQUINAS

Introduction

The highly structured way in which Aquinas develops his philosophy, especially in the *Summa Theologica,* is both a help and a hindrance for one attempting to understand what he has to say. It is a help in that his progressive elaboration of questions enables one to easily identify his major premises, and then to see how the various subsequent topics flow from them. The order of topics is most explicit.[1]

However, in this very method there lies a hidden trap, for one might mistakenly believe that the specific questions to be discussed are simply deduced from the major premises as corollaries. If one believes this to be Aquinas' method, then he will surely miss his profound treatment of the specific subject matter of the questions themselves. To assume that Aquinas merely deduces specific moral conclusions from his general principles will surely hinder one's understanding of what Aquinas' moral reasoning at- to accomplish; for Aquinas deals with these specific questions in terms of the unique factors they involve. Furthermore, Aquinas himself pointed out that the relation between premises and conclusions is much more tenuous in practical reason than in theoretical resaon.[2]

In examining his treatment of the specific moral question of suicide in this chapter, I will try to clarify the implications of Aquinas' threefold prohibition of suicide first in and of themselves, and then to show how his earlier treatments of the principles involved, and the treatment of them by his predecessors, throw light on the *Summa Theologica,* II-II, question 64, article 5.

The treatment of the question, then, will concentrate on Aquinas' response to the question: "Whether one is permitted to kill himself?"[3]

His reasoning results in the conclusion of an absolute prohibition.[4] He also presents five objections to this prohibition and in his responses he attempts to overrule all of them. The very number of objections is in itself significant, for Aquinas usually raises three objections in his articles in the *Summa Theologica*. The larger number of objections seems to indicate both the importance and the complexity of the problem in his eyes.

In the response, Aquinas deals with suicide in terms of three human relationships: that of a person with himself, that of a person with society, and that of a person with God. If one looks at the five objections and their respective responses he will soon notice that they can be subsumed under one or another of the three divisions within the response to the question. Hence, the first and second objections concern justice, which pertains to the relationship with society. The third objection, dealing as it does with sin, would seem to concern the relationship with God; however, if one examines the response to it carefully he will notice that in addition to the distinction between human and divine authority, and the distinction between individual and public authority,[5] also at issue is one's relationship with himself.[6] The fourth objection concerns a seeming contradiction to the prohibition of suicide drawn from the tradition of the Catholic Church. Being a question requiring a theological explanation it concerns man's relationship with God. The fifth objection concerns the quasicourage displayed in certain acts of suicide. This concerns the relationship with one's self.[7]

I shall examine the three parts of the response. First I shall attempt to unfold their meaning by examining various cognate texts and precedents which Aquinas used. Then I shall try to show how each relationship leads into the one succeeding it in Aquinas' discussion, namely, how the relationship with oneself leads into that with society, and how that with society leads into the relationship with God. In other words, the threefold prohibition can be seen in sequence.

2. *The First Argument Against Suicide*

In the first part of the response Aquinas presents the following argument:

> Everything naturally loves itself, the result being that everything naturally keeps itself in being (conservat se in esse), and resists corruptions so far as it can. Wherefore suicide is contrary to the inclination of nature . . . Hence suicide is contrary to the natural law . . .[8]

This answer will require extensive explanation before its intelligibility can be seen. For the question immediately arises: What is natural inclination?

If by natural inclination Aquinas means an empirical state of affairs, then his argument is most inconclusive if not downright misleading. On the surface Aquinas' observation regarding what we now call "the law of self-preservation" appears obvious. Being is something beings strive to maintain, especially living beings who seem to be constantly fighting for life (being) and avoiding death (non-being).[9] This much we all can readily observe. However, the problem begins when Aquinas sees in this generalization a specific moral meaning, namely, therefore one *is to* preserve his life; the converse of which is, therefore one *is not to* destroy his life.

How is the individual's action related to his induction of the general law of self-preservation? At first, it seems as though he might do this in one of two ways.

(1) He can note this general tendency, then note that this is his personal tendency as well, thereafter identifying his own personal desire to live with the general tendency to persist in being. Personal desire sees itself as a part of a general empirical tendency. Nevertheless, this has no moral force because the practical conclusion is only an example of the primary assumption.

(2) On the other hand, one can disconnect his own action from his observation of the general tendency to persist in being. He can note this general tendency, then note that this is not his own personal tendency at all, for example, if he feels self-destructive and has death wishes. Thereafter he sees a distinction between his personal desire to die and the general tendency to persist in being. Personal desire is then taken to be something unique, something radically individuating.[10] The suicidal person might therefore see himself as the exception to a generalization.

Identification with "natural inclination" seems to be rooted in how the individual person feels. If he feels that life is to be affirmed, he will then identify himself with the natural tendency to persist in being. If he feels that life is to be denied, he will then distinguish himself from this natural tendency. The entire connection with natural inclination seems to be circumstantial, and as such either possibility seems to be without moral significance.

One either feels like living or one does not. If he does, the addition of the moral decision to live is superfluous; if he does not, nothing can change the particular state of affairs. In this empirical context natural inclination becomes "general tendency."

However, for empiricists, generalizations are always subsequent to the particular states of affairs they generalize. As such they cannot function as moral principles. The moral principles must be prior to that which it judges, for moral principles must first designate the moral significance of an act *which is to be done or which is to be avoided.*

Thus a moral principle must be prior to the empirical state of affairs to which it is to apply, for if it were subsequent to the state of affairs, if it depended on how the moral subject felt at the time, then at best it would have the force of advice. The desire to persist in being seems to be taken as a general tendency inasmuch as self-destruction is an unusual phenomenon. Nevertheless, the generalization is always *after* the fact, and thus exceptions are always possible and do indeed take place. People choose death; people commit suicide every day. The suicidal person might be "unnatural" in the sense of "unusual," but this is no indication that he is immoral. Feelings, even for Aquinas, are not contingent on the will.[11]

Sidney Hook, in a now famous essay, makes this point most tellingly.

> *Suicide is unnatural.* The word 'unnatural' ought to be stricken out from the pages of our ethical vocabulary. Too many proposals are dismissed with a word whose only intelligible meaning makes it irrelevant to ethical evaluation and whose promiscuous use, empty of any definite or concrete connotation, makes it positively pernicious, blinding those who mouth it to the fact that they have already passed judgment. If 'unnatural' means 'unusual' then courage, sacrifice, temperance, and every other good whose rarity is attested by the fact that it is regarded as an ethical ideal becomes unnatural. What else is meant by the word, save a definite indication of a vague disapproval, is difficult to say. Were it not for the platitudinous vacuity of so much ethical effusion on the subject, one would have to apologize for calling attention to the fact that the descent of the moth into the flame and the precipate bolt of the rabbit into the jaws of the python are as natural as the self-preserving instincts of other creatures.[12]

In short, Hook is reiterating the charge of Hume that it is a modal fallacy to try to deduce "ought" statements from "is" statements, to try to derive values from facts. The charge, when directed against Aquinas, questions the derivation of *contra naturalem legem* from *contra inclinationem naturalem*. The use of "natural" seems ambiguous: as inclination it seems to be an empirical generalization; as law it seems to be a moral principle.

However, it is rash to presume that Aquinas' use of *inclinatio naturalis* makes him a "naturalist" in its currently accepted meaning and thus guilty of a "naturalist fallacy." We must therefore inquire whether natural inclination, or even simply "nature," is, for Aquinas, something more than an empirical generalization. Natural inclination, natural appetency, natural love, and nature itself, all refer to the same thing. The terms are interchangeable for Aquinas.[13]

Generalizability is one of the characteristics of nature. As Aquinas notes in his commentary on the *Nicomachean Ethics*: "What is natural is found in the majority of cases."[14] Nevertheless this is not presented as the essential definition of "natural." The fact that a tendency is found in the majority of cases does not explain why such is indeed the case. Nature is clearly prior to its specific characteristics. Thus Aquinas emphasizes this prior force.

> . . . what belongs to the *purpose of a nature* (finem alicujus naturae) should be something common to the things having that nature, for nature does not fail in what it intends, except in the minority of cases.[15]

Here we are already one step deeper than mere generalization. He is not saying that nature is what is commonly determined by a majority of cases. Rather, he is saying that a majority of cases demonstrate a common determination (or inclination) *because* they are of the same nature. The meaning of *nature* preceded its designation of various states of affairs as *natural*. Thus nature causes what is natural to be such, not vice versa. A nature is discovered through generalization but is not itself that generalization. By establishing an order of precedence we discover that the designation *natural* involves causation.

Consequently, the presence of natural inclination, such as the natural inclination to maintain one's existence, is not something which is accidental; something which *usually* happens but which *may* just as easily not happen. The fact that anything strives to maintain itself in being is due to its very nature operating as a cause. As one commentator observes:

> The idea of movement is fundamental to the concept of *naturalis*

inclinatio. St. Thomas emphasizes that it is not random movement that is involved, but rather, movement of a necessary kind. A being desires what it desires in a manner that accords with it from its own form, with its essential structure.[16]

Now, necessary movement in accordance with a being's form follows from final causality, since beings move towards their own proper ends. Final causality, being necessary and not contingent on the subject's circumstances or even his will, holds up a real good as the proper end of the being's movement. When this real good is understood by practical (moral) reason it contains within itself obligation.[17] That man exists is a theoretical judgment. That man is to maintain his existence is a judgment having moral significance when it is made in any situation where the subject has to make a decision concerning the continuity of his existence. Tendencies and ends are correlative; one cannot be understood without taking the other into immediate consideration.[18] All ends within human life have moral significance for man, the subject of natural (moral) law, provided they are irreducibly good. These *final goods* are the grounds of moral judgments in any situation where a moral decision is called for.

The moral decision to continue to exist is not artificially added to an induction of the fact that the law of self-preservation is effective in a majority of cases.[19] The moral decision is, rather, a practical conclusion based on the truth that life is a good to be pursued. Being the object of natural inclination it is generally operable. As such, the moral judgment of this natural tendency in man includes all pertinent human acts under the appropriate moral rule: being is to be preserved; non-being is to be avoided.[20] Only understanding natural inclination in this way can we see how it is prior to the particular state of one's feelings.

One might very easily at times feel like committing suicide. However, this feeling contradicts life which is a real good. Suicide is unnatural, because it does not intend a real good. Death is a privation of the real good life.[21] The moral consideration of this situation, in the light of the natural inclination to preserve life, is to subordinate the suicidal feeling to human nature. Suicidal feelings are not empirically denied, but, they are denied human value inasmuch as they deprive man of his proper end which is a real good. This consideration will lead to the conclusion that there is no moral justification for suicide. When the teleological thrust of natural inclination is understood, we see that it is not identical with a state of feeling or even a particular action.[22] It is prior to them because of the real priority of its object.

The priority of natural inclination can best be seen when it functions as the presupposition for acts ultimately seen as suicidal. For example, intemperate acts can be prohibited in that they contradict the inclination to life. In the example of temperance the natural presupposition is: *Life is to be protected not endangered.* This is like saying to an alcoholic: "If you don't stop drinking you will surely die of cirrhosis of the liver!" Along these lines Aquinas states: "An individual person may be considered . . . with regard to himself, and thus, if he inflicts an injury on himself, it may come under the head of some kind of sin, in temperance, for instance, or imprudence . . ." [23] Thus the inclination to persist in being is presupposed by the prohibition of acts ultimately understood as self-destructive.

It should be noted that in the *Summa Theologica* II-II, question 94, article 2, the natural inclination to preserve life is presented as one of the first principles of natural law. These principles are taken to be self-evident in the sense that they are irreducible, as this commentator points out.

> Self-evidence in fact has two aspects. On the one hand, a principle is not self-evident if it can be derived from some prior principle, which provides a foundation for it. On the other hand, a principle is not useful as a starting point of inquiry and as a limit of proof unless its underivability is known. The objective aspect of self-evidence, underivability, depends upon the lack of a middle term which might connect the subject and predicate of the principle and supply the cause of its truth. In other words, the reason for the truth of the self-evident principle is what is directly signified by it, not any extrinsic cause.[24]

This aspect of human nature, being a first principle of natural law, is unchangeable.[25] Along these lines, the very primacy of such a thing as "death-wishes" [26] is disputed. Suicide is taken to be a subsequent contradiction of an inclination basically present in everyone.

The suicidal person is not suicidal because *his* natural inclination is *not* to persist in being, rather, he is suicidal because he has circumvented *the* natural inclination already present. For example, he might have decided that the avoidance of pain takes precedence over the inclination to continue in life.[27] In situations such as this practical wisdom (prudentia)

is called for. This seems to be why Aquinas has referred to acts of ultimate self-destruction as being either intemperate or contrary to practical
wisdom.

The virtues, for example, temperance and practical wisdom, dispose
man to act in accordance with the principles of natural law.[28] Virtue, being
a subjective disposition, can be negated by a corrupt or vicious life. However, the inclinations of natural law, which intend real objects, cannot be
negated; one can only be alienated from them, that is, be deprived of them
by vice. Thus an unjust person has negated his subjective virtue of justice,
but he has only alienated himself from society. The social inclination intends a real object, society. It remains, even though justice, which is the
proper disposition for it, has been negated by the individual. So, also, a
blasphemous man has negated his subjective virtue of faith, but he has only
alienated himself from the reality of God by perverting his natural religious
inclination.

The task of moral reasoning is to make these privations apparent by
showing the inconsistency of vice. Intemperance or the lack of practical
wisdom illuminates the relation between the irreducible natural inclination
and the act of suicide.[29] Aquinas continually refers to the persistence of
this inclination in several other cases.[30]

In the case of suicide, that is, *immediate* as opposed to ultimate
self-destruction, the following question must be asked: Does the suicidal
person desire non-being or simply the elimination of his own depressing,
unfortunate, life situation? Aquinas has difficulty with this question because there are situations where life does become so intolerable that one
could perhaps conclude that the inclination to life has been so frustrated
as to be, for all practical purposes, destroyed. In other words, perhaps it
can be argued here that this is not a question of the absence of virtue,
namely, the subjective disposition to natural law, but, rather, the absence
of the principle of natural law itself, namely, the objective moral ground,
in this case the irreducible value of life. And yet despite this possibility,
Aquinas insists on the objective value of life no matter how diminished
it might appear in any particular, subjective situation. The following text
indicates how Aquinas struggled with this problem.

> . . . the Philosopher says: 'To be is delightful to all things.' (*Nico-
> machean Ethics* 1168a5-7) But we are not to understand an evil
> and corrupt life or a sorrowful one, for this is evil simply and is
> simply to be shunned, *though it is appetible in a certain respect.* In

the matter of seeking and shunning, it is all of a piece for a thing to be good and to be destructive of good. Hence we call the very lack of evil a good, as the Philosopher points out (*Nicomachean Ethics* 1172b20). Non-existence therefore assumes the aspect of a good in a state of sorrow or wickedness, which is simple evil, *although it is good in some respect*. In this sense non-existence can be desired under the aspect of good.[31]

This is an answer to the objection that damned souls in hell desire non-existence. On this point Aquinas' teacher, Albert the Great, has set precedence.

> The connection of all this with natural appetency he [Albert] makes explicit in his answers to several objections. He points out, for example, that one who contemplates suicide does not will non-existence or evil but only the termination of his troubled existence; what is the real object of his natural appetite is a good—untroubled existence.[32]

Aquinas seems to follow Albert on this difficult point. No one, for him, really chooses non-being per se; examination will show that the suicidal person has chosen relative non-being. It would seem that any therapeutic treatment of the suicidal person would have to hold the same assumption or else it would be futile to attempt to change what cannot be changed. Only dispositions, not inclinations, can be changed.

We have seen that the essence of natural inclination is final causality, for it alone makes an inclination "natural." The very term "natural" only makes sense when used as a term of distinction. If "natural" were the equivalent of "phenomenal," as its non-teleological use eventually came to mean, then every object of experience would be "natural." [33] Without teleology the term loses its distinctive quality and becomes imprecise to the point of being meaningless. Only understanding the distinguishing function of the term "natural" enables the judgment "suicide is unnatural" to have meaning. Suicide is inconsistent with the preservative tendency in human life, whose reality is insured because of the reality of the end it intends, with or without the cooperation of the free subject. It is because of its illusionary teleology that suicide is *unnatural*.

However, final causality or teleology can be understood in two ways: (1) immanent teleology where we need look no farther than the inner dynamics of the being itself to discover the intelligibility of its now natural tendencies towards specific ends;[34] (2) transcendent teleology where a design is seen as imposed on material by an external mind. The first type of teleology is that presented by Aristotle in the *Nicomachean Ethics* as regards man, and in the *Physics* and the *Metaphysics* as regards the universe.[35] The second kind of teleology is seen in a number of philosophers who preceded Aquinas[36] and is that which Aquinas himself presented in his fifth proof of God's existence, i.e. the "argument from governance of the world." [37] In the first kind of teleology God's relationship with the world need not be taken into immediate consideration. However, in the second kind of teleology, we are directly confronted with God's relationship with the world. As Gilson aptly notes:

> Being absolute such a cause is self-sufficient; if it creates not only being but order, it must be something which at least eminently contains the only principle of order known to us in experience, namely, thought. Now an absolute, self-subsisting, and knowing cause is not an It but a He.[88]

Nevertheless, these two types of teleology are not mutually exclusive. The transcendent type of teleology includes all the intelligibility of the immanent type, plus it involves us with the creative power and wisdom of God. In our specific case, this second type is important to bear in mind, because even prior to the grounding of the suicide prohibition in natural inclination as manifest in human experience, the prohibition is grounded in the creative act of God. Thus in one place Aquinas writes:

> The reason behind these statements is that existence is something chosen (quia omnibus hominibus est eligibile) and cherished by everyone.[39]

In another place he writes:

> Accordingly since all things are destined and directed by God to good, and this is done in such a way that in each one is a principle by which it tends of itself to good as if seeking good itself, it is necessary to say that all things naturally tend to good . . . in virtue of an innate principle all things are said to tend to good as if reaching for it of their own accord.[40]

It is clear that the first quote refers to immanent teleology and the second to transcendent teleology. Moreover, it cannot be argued that the first quote refers to human inclinations, whereas the second refers to subhuman inclinations. On the question of suicide Aquinas is referring to the same natural inclination which subsists in all beings, human or not.[41] The human possession of intellect and will does not alter the all-pervasiveness of this natural inclination.[42]

Now, the transcendent direction of natural inclination by God throws further light on the first part of Aquinas' response to the question of suicide, that is, suicide in the light of the relationship with oneself. For the first argument in Aquinas' response is really two responses. The first part of it takes about natural inclination according to the ability of the subject to *maintain itself* (conservat se) in being. This is, as we have seen, on the level of immanent teleology. However, the second part of the first argument says: ". . . suicide is contrary to charity whereby man ought to love himself. Hence suicide is always a mortal sin, as being contrary . . . to charity." [43] Here love of self, which is seen as the reason for avoiding suicide by nature[44] is also ascribed to charity, the foremost theological virtue.[45] Suicide, then, becomes not only a rejection of man's love for himself but of God's love for man. Charity is rooted in a transcendent teleology.

In order to see how charity can pass moral judgment on suicide, we must examine what Aquinas means by it.

> Accordingly, since there is a communication between man and God, inasmuch as He communicates His happiness to us, some kind of friendship must needs be based on this same communication, of which it is written (I Cor. i.9): God is faithful by Whom you are called unto the fellowship of His son. The love which is based on this communication is charity: wherefore it is evident that charity is the friendship of man for God.[46]

This treatment of charity, especially its quotation from the New Testament about Christ, clearly refers to a relationship with God in the context of Christian revelation. One can only love that which he has confronted in some way. The desire to know the truth about God is a natural inclination, but the actual love of God (caritas) presupposes some concrete revelation of God to man. For Aquinas as a Christian theologian, Christ would constitute this revelation, being, in Christian theology, the incarnation of God,

the second person of the trinity. Charity involves man in a concrete relationship with God as creator of all being. This concreteness cannot be
instituted by natural powers.

> God is loved as the principle of good, on which the love of
> charity is founded; while man out of charity loves himself by reason
> of his fellowship in that God.[47]

Indeed in his response to the first objection, where Aquinas again states the
relationship with self, natural inclination is not even mentioned. He only
mentions charity.[48] The theological interpreters of Aquinas lay greatest
emphasis on charity.[49]

The close connection between charity and natural inclination is ob-
served in other contexts as well. Aquinas sees an essentially teleological
character in both, thus making them closely analogous one to the other.[50]
Charity enables man to reach an end that he desires but may not have the
natural capacity to attain. Thus the difference between charity and natural
inclination is not as to their form; both are causative in the sense of final
causality; both function connaturally with the ends they seek. Indeed the
inclination of nature is even termed "divine" by Aquinas.

> . . . all things have in themselves something divine, that is, an inclina-
> tion of nature which is derived from the first principle—or even their
> (substantial) form itself which is the basis of the inclination.[51]

Their difference is due to their intensity and duration. Charity complements
natural inclination because it improves upon natural inclination in the sense
of grace improving upon nature.[52] Aquinas notes charity's greater power.

> But it is evident that the act of charity surpasses the nature of the
> power of the will, so that, therefore, unless some form be super-added
> to the natural power, inclining it to the act of love, this same act
> would be less perfect than the natural acts and the acts of the other
> powers; nor would it be easy and pleasurable to perform.[53]

If, in Christian theology, grace is needed because original sin damaged
nature, then the greatest need for grace might well be the charity required
to counteract that most unnatural act, self-destruction.[54]

3. *The Third Objection.*

Although there are some difficulties in applying the natural inclination to persist in being to the actual act of suicide, Aquinas has established its clear priority as an inclination. In his general ennunciation of the first principles of natural law (*Summa Theologica* I-II 94.2) and here in his specific discussion of the immorality of suicide, he has chosen to present the natural inclination to persist in being first. This is not only because this inclination is the most general, predicted as it is of all beings. In both contexts, it should be recalled, he is discussing natural inclination in the sense of human nature. Rather, it would seem that Aquinas presents it first because the first relationship is with oneself in that the self is most proximate. Thus the self-evidence of self-love is first in our experience.[55] This proximity to self is partly what is involved in the third objection.

> It is lawful for a man to suffer spontaneously a lesser danger that he may avoid a greater: thus it is lawful for a man to cut off a decayed limb even from himself, that he may save his whole body. Now sometimes a man, by kiling himself, avoids a greater evil, for example an unhappy life or the shame of sin.

In his response to this objection Aquinas first distinguishes between human and divine authority.[56] This will be taken up when I deal with the third part of the prohibition of suicide, that is, the obligation to God. The question of an "unhappy life" (*miseram vitam*) is not taken to mean the unhappy circumstances of a particular life, but rather the general unhappiness of life in this world compared to the bliss of the next. The transition from this world to the next is not so much a part of one's relationship with himself as it is part of the relationship with God. The unhappiness with which the objection deals, from looking at the response to it, is clearly external to a person's particular action. If he should commit suicide because of this unhappiness the act itself constitutes a rejection of the authority of God.

Then again, suicide as self-determined punishment for a sin one has already committed involves the question of public authority in that the punishment of wrongdoers belongs to the domain of public authority as seen from the reply to the second objection. Public authority, is of course

involved in the relationship with society. To commit suicide because of
past wrongs is to usurp this domain.

To commit suicide in order to prevent oneself from sinning is part
of the relationship with self in that it is the result of one's own personal
judgment about himself. One looks upon himself as *one inclined to sin.*
Thus Aquinas says:

> Again it is unlawful for a woman to kill herself lest she be
> violated, because she ought not to commit on herself the very great
> sin of suicide to avoid the lesser sin of another . . . Now it is evident
> that fornication and adultery are less grevious sins than taking a
> man's, especially his own, life: since the latter is most grevious, be-
> cause one injures oneself, to whom one owes the greatest love (cui
> maximam dilectionem debet) . . . his own life for fear he should
> consent to sin, because *evil must not de done that* good may come
> (Rom. iii, 8) or that evil may be avoided.

This part of the response to the objection brings out a further aspect
of the natural inclination to being, namely, it consciously manifests itself
in one's love of self. Furthermore, one loves himself first and foremost
as he is present. This priority of self-love as a present factor means that
one is not to negate the present for fear of what the future might bring,
even out of fear of his own possible future sin which is an act resulting
from one's own moral agency. The presence of the natural inclination to
persist in being is the presupposition for the priority of one's present over
his future in moral judgment. This is the case because the recognition of
this natural inclination as it consciously manifests itself in self-love indicates that the self *as is* is the first object of moral experience. The self
now is not a part of the self *to be* so that it might be sacrificed for it, in
the sense that a diseased limb is part of the whole body and may be thus
sacrificed for it if need be.[57]

That is why suicide per se, which is the most radical self-rejection, is
not permitted by authentic positive law (namely, just social legislation)
nor by the revealed law of God.[58] Moreover, what we have learned from
this part of the response to the objection is that the relationship with self
is even prior to any projection of what the self might do in the future. A
project is subsequent to the *projecting self.* In the case of suicide as a
moral preventive action the principle becomes what was expressed in the
words of Augustine:

But in any case, if for a man to kill himself is also a detestable crime and a damnable sin, as the truth clearly proclaims, who is so mad as to say, "Let us sin now at once, lest we chance to sin later; let us now at once commit murder lest we chance to fall into adultery later.'[59]

4. *The Fifth Objection.*

Furthermore, this priority of the natural inclination to being, as first made consciously manifest in the love of self, excludes sacrifice of the self *as is for* the sake of what the self *might experience* in the future. For this is what is at issue in the fifth objection:

Further, it is related (2 Mach. xiv. 42) that a certain Razias killed himself. Choosing to die nobly rather than to fall into the hands of the wicked, and to suffer abuses unbecoming his noble birth. Now nothing that is done nobly and bravely is unlawful. Therefore suicide is not unlawful.

Aquinas' response is twofold:

It belongs to fortitude that a man does not shrink from being slain by another, for the sake of the good of virtue (propter bonum virtutis), and that he may avoid sin. But that a man take his own life in order to avoid penal evils has indeed an appearance of fortitude (habet quidem quandam speciem fortitudinis) . . . yet it is not true fortitude but rather a weakness of soul unable to bear penal evils, as the Philosopher (*Ethic.* iii.7) and Augustine (*De Civ. Dei* i.22, 23) declare.

In the first part of the response to the objection Aquinas discusses the relation of the specific virtue of courage[60] to virtue in general. The specific virtue is for the sake of the latter. As in all of Aquinas' discussions of relations the order of precedence determines the nature of the relation. This is brought out elsewhere where he defines courage in relation to the genus, virtue.

Wherefore it belongs to human virtue to make man good, to make his work accord with reason (secundum rationem esse). This happens

in three ways: first, by rectifying reason itself, and this is done by the
intellectual virtues; secondly, by establishing the rectitude of reason
in human affairs, and this belongs to justice; thirdly, by removing the
obstacles (impedimenta) to the establishment of this rectitude in human
affairs. Now the human will be hindered . . . from following the rectitude of reason . . . through . . . being disinclined (repellit) to follow
that which is in accordance with reason, on account of some difficulty
that presents itself. In order to remove this obstacle fortitude of the
mind is requisite . . .[61]

Two important points emerge from this text. First, virtue is for the
sake of reason. For Aquinas, reason in human practical context is the
natural law.[62] Therefore, the function of virtue is to dispose man to act in
accordance with the principles of natural law. Virtue is thus subsequent to
natural law.[63] Moreover, courage, although having its own special domain,
cannot contradict that to which it is subsequent. No virtue, by definition,
can contradict a principle of natural law. If it did, it would cease to be a
virtue.

To risk one's life for the good of virtue is acceptable as an act of
the virtue of courage. To rule this out would be to rule out the very
domain of courage. The subsequent relationship with society involves the
risk of being killed in battle while doing one's duty on behalf of the
common good.[64] The subsequent relationship with God involves the risk
of being killed as a martyr.[65] Nevertheless, in both of these cases the fact
of being killed is accidental to the act of doing one's civic or religious
duty.[66] However, to take one's own life in the name of courage is to
contradict the principle of natural law: *Res naturaliter conservat se in
esse et corrumpentibut resistit quantum potest.* A virtue which contradicts the natural law is, for Aquinas, no virtue at all.[67] Therefore, on the
level of virtue itself courage involving actual suicide is excluded from
being considered virtuous.[68]

Furthermore, the particular example chosen in the objection, that of
Razias, brings out this contradiction in particular. If courage means per-
severence in the face of mortal danger, then suicide because of fear of
future troubles is the exact opposite of courage; it is an act of cowardice.
Thus we see from the two parts of the reply both that the virtues in general
cannot contradict the principles of natural law and that the specific virtues
cannot be invoked to justify what turn out to be, on close consideration,
their own specific contradictions.

In concluding this discussion of the responses to the objections which may be subsumed under the discussion of suicide in the context of the relationship with the self, it would be useful to quote Augustine. Much of what Aquinas says about self-love (although not about natural inclination, which is a more original development of his) is Augustinian in a rather straightforward way. Thus Augustine says in this context:

> As it is wicked to say this viz., let us commit suicide lest we sin so it is wicked, surely, to kill oneself. For if there could be any legitimate reason for committing suicide, there could be none more legitimate than this, I am sure. But since not even this one is legitimate, therefore there is none such.[69]

The force of Augustine's remarks is a fortiori. If suicide to avoid sin is the best justification for suicide, because it is an act to save one from himself and even that is not sufficient reason to sanction it, then certainly suicide to avoid pain or disgrace cannot justify itself, for this would be an act to save oneself from something extrinsic to the soul.[70]

5. The Second Argument Against Suicide.

In the second argument of his response Aquinas says:

> Secondly, because every part as such belongs to the whole (est totius). Now every man is part of the community (pars communitatis), and so, as such, he belongs to the community (est communitàtis). Hence by killing himself he injures the community, as the Philosopher declares (Ethic. v.11).[71]

Here Aquinas is discussing suicide in the context of one's relationship with fellow humans in society; he is basing his discussion of the social significance of suicide on the position of Aristotle. Therefore, in my analysis of this second part of the argument against suicide, I shall first present the argument of Aristotle in the fifth book of the *Nicomachean Ethics* and then present Aquinas' exegesis on Aristotle's social philosophy as found in his commentary on that work. Aquinas' social philosophy is an elaboration on Aristotle's. However, the elaboration on one philosopher's work by another will surely lead to some new insights into the topic under discussion.

In the case at hand, Aquinas elaborating on Aristotle's argument against suicide, we will see that Aquinas' responses to the questions raised in the first two objections and his treatment of natural inclination develop issues not explicitly found in Aristole. It is in this response, and the issues developed there and elsewhere, that we will find some original contributions of Aquinas to social philosophy in general and the social significance of suicide specifically. In this response itself Aquinas is rather uncritical of Aristotle's position despite its obvious difficulties.

Aristotle raises the issue at the very end of his treatment of justice.

> The foregoing discussion has indicated the answer to the question, Is it possible or not for a man to commit injustice against himself? One class of just actions consists of those acts, in accordance with any virtue, which are ordained by law. (For instance, the law does not expressly sanction, it forbids) . . . But he who kills himself in a fit of passion, voluntarily does an injury (against right principle) which the law does not allow. Therefore the suicide commits injustice; but against whom? It seems to be against the state rather than against himself; for he suffers voluntarily, and nobody suffers injustice voluntarily. This is why the state exacts a penalty; suicide is punished by certain marks of dishonour, as being an offense against the state.[72]

Aristotle considers suicide, then, to be contrary to the person's relationship with society. The assumption behind this prohibition is that just as the whole is prior to any of its parts, so the state has authority over its individual members. Therefore, no one has the right to rob the state of any of its property, even of his own life. This is what Aquinas emphasizes as Aristotle's meaning. However, in order to see how this assumption is an intelligible basis for Aquinas' unequivocal prohibition of suicide, we must inquire just how a person is a "part" of the state and how suicide "injures" the state.

Reflection will surely indicate that this assumption, at face value, could lead to the opposite conclusion, namely, it could almost as easily be the basis for the permission or even the injunction of suicide. This conclusion could be drawn by the individual himself or the state in the person of its public officials.

For example, let us suppose that I am a chronically ill pauper living on public assistance in a state institution. I am also a patriot who values his citizenship. Now I happen to read in the newspaper that the governor of the state has publically declared that the state in on the verge of bankruptcy because of the ever increasing welfare rolls. The only solution to the problem is to increase the number of taxpayers. An appeal is made to every patriotic welfare recipient to get off the welfare rolls and onto the tax rolls by obtaining a job. If the trend is not reversed, the governor emphasizes, the state will go bankrupt and civil society in the state will be in serious jeopardy inasmuch as all necessary services (for example, police protection) will be curtailed for lack of funds. I listen to all of this most intently as any patriot who respects public authority would do. I see the problem, but I also know that my physical condition precludes my ever becoming a taxpayer. As long as I live I will be a drain on the state. Therefore, I conclude that the only way I can do my patriotic duty to get off the welfare rolls is to kill myself.

If this story sounds purely imaginative, then one need only be reminded that many suicide notes read something like this: "I am of no use to anybody. You will all be better off without me. I am killing myself because this is the right thing to do. I cannot bear to be a burden. Please understand."

In other words, if the quality of the relationship between the individual human person and society is determined by considerations of usefulness, then the morality of suicide will be totally contingent on whether the person who commits suicide is useful or not. In this context, it would be immoral for a sentry guarding the entrance to the city to commit suicide and endanger every one of the citizens; or for a father of five small children to commit suicide thereby leaving his family helpless and without support. However, it is moral, following this line of thought, for a chronically ill pauper to commit suicide so as to "contribute" the cost of his continued maintenance to society; or for an elderly parent to commit suicide so as to enable his children to apply what his own continued care would cost towards a college education for his academically promising grandchild. In the latter context, suicide would not only be permitted but would actually be heroic. This is how one might easily draw a moral conclusion from the principle that man is part of the state.

Moreover, the state in the persons of its public officials might enjoin suicide on those citizens who do not measure up to the accepted standards of social utility. One need only remember the fates of Socrates in Athens and of Seneca in Rome. This injunction could be either explicit or implicit. In Japanese culture, for example, those who have "lost face" are explicitly encouraged to rid society of their troublesome presence by *harikiri*.

Suicide might also be seen as implicitly endorsed policy in certain social pronouncements. When Hitler declared the subhuman status of the Jews and insisted that their very presence stood in the way of the "New Germany," was he not encouraging suicide long before his "final solution" went into effect? In the world today many public officials declare that the most important social issue is overpopulation, that unless we have fewer people human society will be impossible because there will just not be enough of the basic necessities for everyone. Is this not a tacit suggestion, not only to do such things as legalizing abortion, but also to encourage the "useless" to rid society of their uselessness? How could this social philosophy be the basis for a categorical condemnation of suicide? We are especially suspicious of this type of reasoning because contemporary events have shown us some of the monstrous results which follow from assuming that man is "part" of his society. All of this is brought out by Sidney Hook.

But we may counter with a more direct and effective response. Far from being a crime against society, suicide may actually further the welfare of society. The logic of utilitarian ethics inevitably leads to this position, to the surprise of a number of its adherents. The greatest good or happiness of the greatest number may sometimes at attained by personal sacrifice, as the annals of heroism and martyrdom will attest . . . it is not altogether inconceivable that sometimes refusal to commit suicide would constitute a crime against society.[73]

The fact that man is part of society is a notion Aquinas emphasized many times. The subordination of parts to the whole is something which permeates all nature, both human and non-human .

For, since one man is a part of the community, each man in all that he is or has belongs to the community, just as a part in all that it is, belongs to the whole. So too, nature inflicts a loss on the part in order to save the whole.[74]

This is why all acts of virtue refer to justice, because justice pertains to the human whole (society), whereas the other virtues only pertain to the human part (the individual).[75] Although in the article explicitly devoted to suicide Aquinas does consider its meaning for the individual himself, as we have seen; in another context he skips over this and emphasizes suicide's meaning solely as injustice to the state and to God.[76]

However much Aquinas may favor the part-whole analogy, it does not by any means exhaust his understanding of man's relationship with society. It is relative to other aspects of sociality. Once we see that this analogy does not prevent us from regarding other aspects of human sociality, we will then be able to see that whereas a person's loyalty to the state as one of its constituents prevents one from commiting suicide, an act of irrevocable desertion, this same loyalty cannot require that one commit suicide, an act of irrevocable sacrifice.

Loyalty to the state by remaining steadfast in service (that is, staying alive) does not exhaust human nature inasmuch as authentic social participation does not constitute or attempt to constitute man's full nature. Sacrifice to the state, by committing what Durkheim called "altruistic suicide," [77] does indeed exhaust human nature inasmuch as it radically reduces human sociality to political subservience. We shall see that the roots of human sociality antecede political obedience; the dynamics of political life, seen more fully, place it in proper perspective; and the fullness of human sociality transcends the limits of the city of man. Only by taking these three points into consideration can we see how Aquinas' use of the part-whole analogy by no means makes him a "collectivist" or a "social utilitarian," as these labels are currently interpreted.

To say that the roots of human sociality antecede human participation in social life as a part thereof means that the person is not the complete product of society. He does not come to society empty. Thus society's claims on him must be consistent with his antecedent constitution, that is, with human nature. Social life is a real relation between two distinct entities: the person and society. In order for the relation to be authentic, then, the respective natures of these two distinct entities must be respected. This is brought out most immediately, for our purposes, when Aquinas comments on Aristotle's prohibition of suicide. As I pointed out when I presented that passage from the Nicomachean Ethics, Aristotle is not very clear on the rationale for the prohibition. Is the demand of the state for what might be called "existential loyalty" a conclusion drawn from the state's own positive authority over its constituent parts; or is the demand for this loyalty drawn from something prior to the state's own positive authority? Aristotle himself is most unclear on questions of natural law (that is, "right reason").[78]

Where Aristotle is vague, Aquinas is more certain.

In no case does the law command a man to take his own life. But those acts that the law does not command as just, it forbids as unjust. This is not to be understood as if no mean exists between the command and the prohibition of the law, since there are many acts that are neither commanded nor forbidden by the law but are left to man's will, for example, buying or not buying a particular thing. But this is to be understood in the sense that *it is only those things which are forbidden as unjust in themselves that the law in no case commands.*[79] [Italics mine.]

It is the "things which are forbidden as unjust in themselves" which determine the commandments of the law of the state. The law gives expression to that which has always been right. However much society may improve upon nature, nature is always antecedent to it and thus limits it in advance. The law of the state cannot, therefore, contradict the natural law. As often as Aquinas emphasizes that one is a part of the social whole even more does he emphasize the priority of natural law over any unjust decree of the state. Human rights stem from nature. No matter how much one may be subordinate to the state, this is *because* of his nature which intends participation in society. Thus Aquinas says:

> Consequently, every human law has just so much of the nature of law as it is derived from the law of nature. But if in any point it departs from the law of nature, it is no longer a law but a perversion of law.[80]

This statement of Aquinas has had tremendous influence on much current social theory which is concerned with human rights in the face of the power of the state in modern society.

Nevertheless, we must now inquire just how nature is prior to human society so as to give natural law precedence over the positive law of the state. It is not enough to say that the person is manifest as part of nature before he becomes part of society, taking as our example the fact that an infant is closer to the realm of nature, being guided by unconscious impulse, than it is to the social realm, lacking as it does rational communication. For in this case nature is a mere potentiality to society and can hardly be seen as having anything but temporal priority.

Therefore, in order to see *priority* in the antecedent status of nature, we must see natural law operating in truly human perspective *before* the social relation is constituted. This can only be done when we understand the natural inclination to live as constituting the person's most immediate relationship with himself, as we did when we dealt with Aquinas' first argument against suicide.

This relationship, having a self-contained domain to be sure, nevertheless intends the subsequent relationship with society inasmuch as the relationship with self does not imply self-sufficiency. Man is by nature a social animal, for Aquinas, because his natural inclination to life intends a uniquely human, that is social, fulfillment.[81] This is why both Aristotle and Aquinas refuse to see the relationship with the self as actually pertaining to justice, the social virtue.[82]

All of this sounds very Aristotelian. However, Aquinas' treatment of the natural inclination to persist in being limits the authority of society to that of a means for human fulfillment. If society attempts to go beyond that limit, if it attempts to make its own demands absolute, then society has forfeited nature's intention. If one did not have an enduring relationship with himself, then society would wholly eclipse human nature, as in the later position of Hobbes. If, on the other hand, the relationship with the self were complete, self-sufficient and self-fulfilling, then sociality would be reduced to a function of individual projection, as in the later position of Locke. Aquinas' position, as a number of commentators have shown, avoids these two extremes.[83] Neither natural inclination nor sociality contradict each other. However, if the human person held that natural inclination precluded sociality, he would thereby be frustrating natural inclination's own intent. If, on the other hand, he held that sociality demanded the rejection of natural inclination, then he would thereby be eclipsing nature's mandate for social fulfillment. The first case would destroy the relation with society by privation; the second would destroy it by excess.

Aquinas' originality, therefore, consists in explicating the meaning of natural inclination in human context. By doing so, his presentation of sociality involves an equilateral understanding of both the realm of nature and the realm of society, and it makes the relation between them a genuine interaction. In Aristotle all of this is vague and undeveloped. Hence society has no right to require suicide of any of its citizens. This is how the fact that man is "part" of the community cannot lead to the permission or injunction of suicide in any case whatsoever.[84]

Understanding the natural antecedents to sociality has enabled us to deny that any act of suicide is sanctioned by participation in society. This has been done by showing what sociality is not. This is also shown within the very article concerning suicide. In the third objection, the part-whole analogy is put forth as a possible basis for sanctioning suicide in a specific situation. Even though Aquinas does not explicitly discredit the analogy in his response to the objection, his response certainly implies such a rejection of the logic of the objection.

The person is part of the community in a uniquely human way. The relation with the community is bilateral: the person owes the community loyalty and service *in return* for the just distribution of society's goods he has received.

> Now a twofold order may be considered in relation to a part . . . In the second place there is the order of the whole towards the parts, to which corresponds the order of that which belongs to the community in relation to each single person. This order is directed by distributive justice, which distributes common goods proportionately.[85]

Obviously the notion of *redistribution* could not be applied in the relation of an individual animal to his species or of a part to the overall machine.[86] In these relations the movement is all one way.

If the common good is the end of human society, and if that good is human happiness, it is impossible to imagine the common good being real without a proportionate distribution among all those persons who commune therein. The common good is not the "collective good." The achievement of the common good to any extent can only take place where society is a true communion of persons. There is no such thing as a happy society without happy citizens. Suicide is a crime against this communion in which even the suicidal person himself shares on an equal basis.[87]

No matter how much private agony suicide seems to allieviate, it is ultimately contrary to true human happiness which lies in communion, even if no usefulness is involved. In a true communion of persons one can see a need for even the helpless and infirm. Their very presence enables us to practice the human virtues of benevolence and generosity. This conception of society has had an attraction, as a reason for judging suicide to be immoral, for many thinkers who in other respects are far removed from the general philosophical position of Aquinas.[88]

Furthermore, the intent of human sociality transcends the limits of the part-whole relationship with society. The human is more than a social animal. This does not imply a diremption between sociality and something higher within him. Rather, it means that for Aquinas man's very sociality intends more than its manifestation in the city of man. Thus he actually connects the two in an upward gradation.

Certainly it is part of that love which should exist among men that a man preserve the good even of a single human being. But it is much better and more divine that this be done for a whole people and for states. It is even sometimes desirable that this be done for one state only, but it is much more divine that it be done for a whole people that includes many states. *This is said to be more divine because it shows greater likeness to God who is the ultimate cause of all good.*[89] [Italics mine.]

The natural inclination to persist in being, which we have discussed earlier, functions as both a source and a limit on human sociality: it is what the person brings to society and what society is bound to respect. It is antecedent to sociality. The relationship with God, from the other side as it were, transcends sociality. However, unlike Augustine who makes the city of man antithetical to the city of God,[90] Aquinas makes the city of man (human society) intend the city of God (that is, the state of friendship with God). Hence the relationship with God functions both as a fulfillment and as a limit on human sociality. Aquinas emphasizes this:

Man is not ordained to the body politic according to all that he is and has; and so it does not follow that every act of his acquires merit or demerit in relation to the body politic. But all that man is, and can, and has, must be referred to God; and therefore every act of man, whether good or bad, acquires merit or demerit in the sight of God from the fact of the act itself.[91]

There is more in human sociality than political involvement. The text from the *Commentary* and that from the *Summa* complement each other. The *Summa* text distinguishes Aquinas from Aristotle inasmuch as Aristotle does not posit an actual human relationship with God.[92] The text from the *Commentary* distinguishes Aquinas from Augustine. However, this will be considered in greater detail in the next section where we deal with suicide in the context of the relationship with God. What must be emphasized here is that society may not eclipse the human relationship with God by making any absolute "existential demands," that is, that a citizen commit suicide.

6. The Second Objection.

Despite the fact that Aquinas most definitely limits the authority of society over the human person,[93] he does hold that the state has the right of capital punishment in specific cases.[94] The second objection pertains to whether self-inflicted capital punishment should be considered as the sin of suicide.

> Further, it is lawful for one who exercises public authority to kill evildoers. Now he who exercises public authority is sometimes an evil-doer. Therefore he may lawfully kill himself.

In his response Aquinas further limits public authority.

> One who exercises public authority may lawfully put to death an evildoer, since he can pass judgment on him. But no man is judge of himself. Wherefore it is not lawful for one who exercises public authority to put himself to death for any sin whatever: although he may lawfully commit himself to the judgment of others.[95]

This is also a point he repeats in his reply to the third objection.[96]

Without getting involved in the question of capital punishment itself, a matter which would take us too far afield, we must nevertheless ask: Why can a public authority pass judgment on others but not on himself?

First, we must understand what is meant by "pass judgment." Obviously it does not mean an intellectual judgment, for if this were the case the conclusion of Aquinas' reply—"He may lawfully commit himself to the judgment of others," would make no sense. The sinner, no matter who he is, knows he has sinned. His limitation, then, is not noetic but judicial. He knows he has sinned, but he may not punish himself for it. Therefore, we must inquire just how Aquinas defines public authority and why that definiation precludes self-punishment.

> Public authority is necessitated by the teleological nature of human society. The common good is the coordinating principle of all activities having social significance. However, this coordination, involving as it does the continued correlation of means and ends, requires a person or persons empowered with the right to make decisions required by these correlations. Because of the diversified number and quality of these correlations, this decision-making authority requires specific persons, a professionalization as it were,—someone to act on behalf of the people. Authority is necessitated by the very diversification inherent in society itself, a diversification calling for continuing coordination for the sake of the common good.[97]

Its presence is not the admission that people are not virtuous enough to determine their own laws.[98] The authorities act on behalf of the people. Their necessity is administrative. Early in the *Treatise on Law* Aquinas states:

> Now to order anything to the common good belongs either to the whole people or to a public personage who has care of the whole people. Hence the making of a law belongs either to the whole people or to a public personage who has care of the whole people; for in all matters the directing of anything to the end concerns him to whom the end belongs.[99]

This definition is elaborated in the treatise on rulership, *De Regimine Principium.*[100]

The public authority is the person *through whom* society acts in the interest of the common good. Thus the public authority must keep his public interest and his private interest separate or else his authority ceases to be public. What is public is determined by what is common. Public authority is only as public as its function on behalf of the common good. For this reason any public acts of public officials not directed to the common good are unjust.[101] Public authority does not alter the private status of the person holding it, because all individuals, no matter what their office, still *participate* in common life; they are never identical with it. If public service obliterated one's private status altogether, then *any* act of a public servant would constitute public authority.

In the case of self-inflicted capital punishment we can see from what I have just said why this involves a perversion of public authority. In this case the public official is acting simultaneously in a twofold capacity: as judge of his act he is a public official; as the subject of his judgment he is a private individual. As such we have a public authority mixing his public and private status in one irrevocable act. This is as much of an appropriation of public authority for private purposes as any other usurpation. Private individuals cannot act in a public capacity unless duly appointed.[102] Within that capacity itself they are no longer private parties. This is why they may not pass legal judgment on themselves. If they recognize themselves as guilty they must turn themselves over to other public authorities for punishment. In so doing they cease to be public authorities and have a solely private status. Of all the aspects of the prohibition of suicide this one is treated in the most legalistic way.

7. *The Third Argument Against Suicide.*

The third argument of Aquinas' response concerns man's relationship with God.

> Thirdly, because life is God's gift to man, and is subject to His power, Who kills and makes to live. Hence whoever takes his own life, sins against God, even as he who kills another's slave, sins against that slave's master, and as he who usurps to himself judgment of a matter not entrusted to him. For it belongs to God alone to pronounce sentence of death and life, according to Deut. xxxii.39, *I will kill and I will make to live.*[103]

The logic employed here is similar to that which Plato used in the *Phaedo,* as we saw in the previous chapter, namely, that the relationship with God is like that of a slave to his master. Suicide, then, is a rejection of the authority of God, who gives being. Life is the property of God; it belongs to him as its creator.

This argument is rooted in Aquinas' most extensive treatment of the causal power of God in the first sections of both the *Summas.* God is the ever-present and ever-necessary cause of all being.[104] There is no independence of any creature from God. This whole relationship of rulership is fundamentally expressed in Aquinas' five ways of proving the existence of God, all of which conclude the supreme and everpresent causality of God.[105] In theoretical reason this demonstrated truth is a necessary conclusion following from the recognition of causal efficacy operating in the world. To admit causal efficacy and to deny the existence of God would be, for Aquinas, a theoretical absurdity. In practical reason no act can be considered the good to be done which at the same time rejects the supreme goodness of God.[106] Suicide, being a rejection of God's most fundamental goodness to the creature, that is, the gift of being itself, can never, therefore, be considered good. For Aquinas this would be a moral absurdity. This is why, for example, capital punishment is not a primary precept of natural law, but must, rather be derived from considerations of self-defense.

All of this is what one would of course expect from a religious thinker like Aquinas, for this approach is basically religious. It has many precedents in religious thought.[107] Many commentators have felt that this is the strongest of the three arguments Aquinas presents for the immorality of suicide.[108] It is the strongest because it has the most extensive grounding in Aquinas' metaphysics.

When we consider the authority of God we are dealing with a notion much more extensively developed by Aquinas than either natural inclination or sociality.[109] Since the human person is not his own creator, the decision as to the termination of his created being is out of his hands. This is emphasized in the very beginning of the reply to the third objection. "Man is made master of himself through his free will: wherefore he can lawfully dispose of himself as to those matters which pertain to this life which is ruled by man's free will."[110] Thus we see that the prohibition of suicide because of the authority of God is rooted in Aquinas' metaphysics and his philosophical anthropology. The metaphysical foundation concerns the absolute priority of God over any of his creatures. The anthropological foundation concerns the difference between human and non-human life. Other creatures may be sacrificed for human use.[111] However, the human himself may never be sacrificed for the use of any other creature, even other humans, or even himself.[112]

Despite the fact that this third foundation for the prohibition of suicide is more intrinsically cogent than the previous two, it must nevertheless be reconciled with two factors Aquinas as a Christian theologian could not very well ignore. The first is raised by the third objection. "Now sometimes a man by killing himself avoids a greater evil, for example, an unhappy life, or the shame of sin. Therefore a man may kill himself." From his reply to this part of the objection it is clear that by "unhappy life" (miseram vitam), Aquinas is not referring to the particular circumstances of a particular life, but rather, to the general unhappiness of life in this world compared to the bliss of life in the next world.

> But the passage from this life to another and happier one is subject not to man's free-will but to the power of God. Hence it is not lawful for man to take his own life that he may pass to a happier life, nor that he may escape any unhappiness whatsoever of the present life, because the ultimate and most fearsome evil of this life is death, as the Philosopher states (*Ethic.* iii.6). Therefore to bring death upon oneself in order to escape the other afflictions of this life, is to adopt a greater evil in order to avoid a lesser.[113]

This is a problem which any believer in the future bliss of the soul after death must face. The problem was Plato's as well. If our end is to enjoy the bliss of the next world, then why can we not bring about the transition ourselves, that is, commit suicide? Aquinas' answer to the question, it seems to me, is similar to Plato's. I am not saying that Plato's conception of God and Aquinas' are similar. They are obviously rooted in different religious traditions and are philosophically developed in different ways. However, this difference is not of immediate issue here, because the problem before us is not about the nature of God but about human nature. For both Plato and Aquinas the human soul is immortal.[114] Furthermore, for both philosophers, true human fulfillment is only found in the beatific vision which can only take place in the immaterial future world.[115] If one knows *that* such is the case, then why wait?

For Aquinas, as for Plato before him, the answer to this question lies in the relation of knowledge to action, namely, what constitutes rational action? It should be recalled from the response that "passage from this life to another and happier one is subject not to man's free will . . . as those matters which pertain to this life . . ." If everything human were taken to be subject to the will of God immediately and exclusively, then any assertion of human will would be contrary to the proper power of God. If, on the other hand, everything human were taken to be subject only to the free will of man, then any assertion of divine will would be contrary to the proper power of the human person. Aquinas' position lies between these two extremes. Human will has its own limited domain.

The limitation of man's will is intrinsically intellectual, namely, man can only properly will *what* he already knows. Since man's knowledge is limited, so also is his rational will. The subordination of will to intellect is a theme extensively developed by Aquinas.

> If therefore the intellect and will be considered with regard to themselves, then the intellect is the higher power . . . For the object of the intellect is the very notion of the appetible good; and the appetible good, the notion of which is in the intellect, is the object of the will. Now the more simple and the more abstract a thing is, the nobler and higher it is in itself; and therefore the object of the intellect is higher than the object of the will.[116]

Because the intellect presents the proper object to the will it is held to move the will formally.[117] Now the intellect is limited to *what* it can experience, and *that* which it can infer from its experience. Having no experience of the future life it does not know *what* it is (quid est), but only *that it is* (an sit). Because the heavenly beatitude consists of the contemplation of God as He is in essence (quid est), our present knowledge of the future life is the same as our present knowledge of God. Aquinas is emphatic that in this life we only know *that* God exists, not *what* He is.[118] The information supplied by the articles of faith does not constitute knowledge.[119] Therefore, the future life is not a proper object of the will. One can believe in it, one can hope for it, but one cannot will it so as to be accomplished by a human act. Aquinas is equally emphatic that only God can bring about man's supernatural fulfillment.[120]

The power of God is the extrinsic limit on the authority of the human will. But since the human will does have its own specific domain, one must understand its intrinsic intellectual limitation before alluding to its extrinsic divine limitation. It is important to remember that when Aquinas, in the beginning of the response to the third objection, seems to be speaking in a theological context, his only reference is to a common sense observation of Aristotle. There Aristotle writes: "Now the most terrible thing of all is death; for it is the end, and when a man is dead, nothing, *we think*, neither good nor evil can befall him any more." [121] Death is, therefore, the greatest evil to be avoided. One can only rationally act upon that which he already knows. Suicide for the sake of the bliss of the future world is not only a sinful usurpation of the proper domain of God, it is even more essentially an irrational act based on no definite knowledge.[122]

All this is in agreement with Plato's argument in the Phaedo, as I have explicated it in the last chapter. However, it is more extensively developed by Aquinas. Aquinas laid a great deal more groundwork for his presentation of the problem; thus he does not struggle with it as much as Plato did.

The second factor which Aquinas as a Christian theologian must reconcile with the prohibition of suicide, as grounded in the authority of God, is the fact that the Catholic Church has honored as saints certain persons who committed suicide. This seems to be a theological endorsement of a specific type of suicide. Thus the fourth objection states:

> Further, Samson killed himself, as related in Judges xvi, and yet he is numbered among the saints (Heb. xi). Therefore it is lawful for a man to kill himself.

Aquinas replies:

> As Augustine says (*De Civ. Dei* i.21), not even Samson is to
> be excused that he crushed himself together with his enemies under
> the ruins of the house, except the Holy Ghost, who had wrought man
> wonders through him, had secretly commanded him to do this. He
> assigns the same reason in the case of certain holy women, who at
> the time of persecution took their own lives, and who are commemo-
> rated by the Church.[123]

In three earlier treatments of the problem of suicide this is Aquinas' sole
concern.[124] This difficulty is the most specifically theological one which
Aquinas takes up in this article, arising as it does from the tradition of the
Catholic Church. Sertillanges is right, I believe, when he wryly notes:
"L'histoire chrétienne présente des faits que Saint Thomas théologien
pourrait trouver embarrasants pour sa thèse." [125]

The only answer to the problem, that is, that it seems that a *Deus ex
machina* can come out of Church tradition and Biblical revelation and
exonorate persons who by considerations of natural factors would be
accounted as sinners, is that the intrusion of supernatural considerations
always takes precedence over the natural considerations. In much the
same way the miraculous is not ascribable to God's action as seen within
the workings of the natural order.[126]

The embarrassment is because, whereas the theological consideration
of charity, for example, perfects the natural inclination to persist in being,
the theological justification of suicidal martyrdom raised here seems to
be working against natural inclination. This is in the last analysis a problem for any natural law theorist who is also a theologian.[127] It is one thing
to see Revelation as transcending the specifically human limits of natural
law in the sense of addition. It is quite another thing to see Revelation
dispensing certain persons from the supposedly immutable precepts of
natural law in the sense of subtraction. The only answer seems to be that
God's will as the source of all being, including natural inclination, takes
precedence in every seeming conflict. What Aquinas accomplished, however, was to isolate these religious precedents to such an extent that one
could not conclude from them a general sanction concerning religiously
motivated suicide.

NOTES

1 "To the philosopher, the most striking quality of the moral science of St. Thomas is its firm foundation in metaphysics . . . As a consequence, it is most difficult to determine the starting point of the moral teaching of the *Summa Theologica*. The progress of thought is continuous and homogeneous. Speculative theology and metaphysics grow into moral theology." Vernon J. Bourke, *St. Thomas and the Greek Moralists* (Milwaukee: Marquette University Press, 1947), p. 8.

2 "For since the speculative reason is concerned chiefly with necessary things, which cannot be otherwise than they are, its proper conclusions, like the universal principles, contain the truth without fail. The practical reason, on the other hand, is concerned with contingent matters, which is the domain of human actions; and consequently, although there is necessity in the common principles, the more we descend towards the particular, the more frequently we encounter defects." *Summa Theologica* I-II, 94.4, trans. from *The Basic Writings of St. Thomas Aquinas* II, ed. Anton C. Pegis (New York: Random House, 1945), p. 777. (Hereafter referred to as "S.T." and "Pegis trans.," respectively).

3 "Utrum alicui liceat seipsum occidere? (Latin text from P. Caramello ed. (Rome: Marietti, 1962). All Latin S. T. quotes from this edition.

4 "Respondeo dicendum quod seipsum occidere est *omnino illicitum* triplici ratione."

5 "Tum etiam quia malefactorem occidere non licet nisi per iudicium *publicae potestatis.*"

6 "*Homo constituitur dominus sui ipsius* per liberum arbitrium . . . sibi ipsi nocet, cui maximam dilectionem debet."

7 ". . . non tamen vera fortitudo, sed magis quaedam *mollities animi* . . ."

8 *S.T.* II-II, 64.5, trans. of the Fathers of the English Dominican Province (London: Burnes, Oates and Washbourne, Ltd., 1922), vol. X, pp. 203-204. (Hereafter referred to as "Dominican edition").

9 "*To live*, accordingly, is nothing else than for a substance with such a nature *to be;* and *life* signifies this very fact, but abstractly . . . Hence, *living* is not an accidental, but a substantial predicate." *S.T.* I, 18.2, Pegis ed. I, p. 189.

10 This was indeed the Stoic point of view which not only tolerated suicide but actually encouraged it. See Epictetus, *Discourses*, I, 24; Seneca, *Epistolae*, 70. Cf. Jean-Paul Sartre, *Being and Nothingness* trans. Hazel Barnes, (Philosophical Library, New York, 1956), pp. 553-556.

11 See *S.T.*, I-II, 17.8.

12 Sidney Hook, "The Ethics of Suicide," *International Journal of Ethics,* 37 (1927), p. 179. Cf. Hume's "Essay on Suicide" (first published in 1898) in Raziel Abelson, *Ethics and Metaethics* (New York: St. Martin's Press, 1963), esp. pp. 113-114.

13 For the pertinent texts showing the identical meaning of all these terms see G. J. Gustafson, *The Theory of Natural Appetency in the Philosophy of St. Thomas* (Washington: Catholic University Press, 1944), esp. pp. 12-13. See also *S.T.* III, 2.1. Cf. D. J. O'Connor, *Aquinas and Natural Law* (New York: Macmillan, 1967), pp. 47-48.

[14] Book IV, lesson 5, trans. C. I. Litzinger, (Chicago: Regnery, 1964), Vol. I, p. 306: "Id autem quod naturale est in pluribus invenitur." Latin text ed. R. M. Spiazzi (Rome: Marietti, 1964).

[15] *Ibid.,* Book I, lesson 14, vol. I, p. 74.

[16] R. A. Armstrong, *Primary and Secondary Precepts in Thomistic Natural Law Teaching* (The Hague: M. Nijhoff, 1966), p. 43.

[17] See L. Thiry, "The Ethical Theory of Saint Thomas," *Journal of Religion,* 50.2 (April, 1970), pp. 175-176.

[18] "The self-evident propositions or axioms which correlate the good and desire not only show that good and desire, like whole and part, are primitive and indefinable terms; the axioms also explicate the meaning of these terms." Mortimer J. Adler, *The Time of Our Lives* (New York: Holt, Rhinehart and Winston, 1970), p. 89.

[19] "This moral system thus puts into place at the outset the concept of 'ought to be', for if this ought to be is not inscribed to begin with in that which is, no artifice of dialectics can put it there." Etienne Gilson, *Moral Values and the Moral Life,* trans. L. R. Ward (St. Louis and London: B. Herder, 1931), p. 88.

[20] "Obligation is a strictly derivative concept, with its origin in ends and the requirements set by ends. If natural law imposes obligations that good acts are to be done, it is only because it primarily imposes with rational necessity that an end must be pursued." Germain G. Grisez, "The First Principle of Practical Reason," *Natural Law Forum,* X (1965), p. 180. See H. A. Rommen, *The Natural Law,* trans. T. R. Hanley, O.S.B. (St. Louis and London: B. Herder, 1947), chap. 3.

[21] For the distinction between negation and privation in moral reasoning see *S.T.* I-II, 85.1, 2, 4.

[22] "And, in fact, *tendency toward* is more basic than *action on account of,* for every active principle tends toward what its action will bring about, but not every tending ability goes into action on account of the object of its tendency. Practical reason, therefore, presupposes good." Grisez, "The First Principle of Practical Reason," pp. 177-178. "The works are obviously means to the goods. And what are the objects of the natural inclination? Not merely morally good acts, but such substantive goods as self-preservation . . . The preservation of human life is certainly a human good. The act which preserves life is not the life preserved . . ." *Ibid.,* p. 184.

[23] *S.T.* II-II, 59.3 ad 2, Domin. ed. X, p. 141. "Imprudence" as a literal translation of *imprudentia* has the misleading connotation in our contemporary usage of "calculative skill," or "cleverness." Therefore, it would seem better to translate it as "practical stupidity."

[24] Grisez, "The First Principle of Practical Reason," p. 173.

[25] "Natural law, so far as it contains common precepts which never fail, does not allow of dispensation." *S.T.* I-II, 97.4 ad 3, Pegis ed. II, p. 805.

[26] The very seminal term was coined by Freud. See *Beyond the Pleasure Principle,* trans. James Strachey (New York: Bantam Books, 1959), pp. 70 ff.

[27] For a discussion on this type of problem, see L. Thiry, "The Ethical Theory of Saint Thomas," pp. 175-176.

[28] See *S.T.* II-II, 123.12.

[29] See *S.T.* II-II, 64.7.

[30] See *In Libros Ethicorum,* Book VII, lesson 1.

[31] *De Veritate,* 22, 1 ad 7, trans. R. W. Schmidt, S.J., *Truth* (Chicago: Regnery, 1954), pp. 38-39. See *S.T.* I, 5.2 ad 3; also Matt. 26:24, 27:5 and Augustine, *De Civitate Dei* I. 17.

32 Gustafson, *The Theory of Natural Appetency in the Philosophy of St. Thomas*, p. 25, referring to I P. *Sum. Theol.* tract VI, mem. i, quaest. 26, art. 2, pt. 1 ad 1 et 2. Cf. Augustine, *De Librio Arbitrio III.* 8

33 "The purpose of the discovery of nature cannot be grasped if one understands by nature 'the totality of phenomena.' For the discovery of nature consists precisely in the splitting-up of that totality into phenomena which are natural and phenomena which are not natural: 'nature' is a term of distinction. Prior to the discovery of nature, the characteristic behavior of anythings or any class of things was conceived of as its custom or its way." Leo Strauss, *Natural Right and History*, p. 82.

34 "Following Aristotle, Saint Thomas used the word 'nature' with many different shades of meaning. Now according to Aristotle 'it is plain that nature in the primary and strict sense is the essence of things which have in themselves, as such, a source of movement.' . . . It follows that, if the word 'nature' means essence with relation to development and growth, a nature is a mode of being which does not possess its state of accomplishment, but is designed to reach it through a progression." Thiry, "The Ethical Theory of Saint Thomas," p. 171.

35 For a fine discussion of the implications of Aristotelian teleology see W. D. Ross, *Aristotle* (New York: Meridian Books, 1960), pp. 181-182.

36 See H. A. Wolfson, *Philo* II (Cambridge, Mass.: Harvard University Press, 1947), pp. 75 ff.

37 *S.T.* I, 2.3.

38 Etienne Gilson, *God and Philosophy* (New Haven: Yale University Press, 1941), p. 140.

39 *In Libros Ethicorum*, Book IX, lesson 9, Litzinger ed., Vol. II, p. 819.

40 *De Ver.*, 22.1, Schmidt ed. III, pp. 36-37. Cf. *ibid.*, ad 2, p. 38; *S.T.* I-II, 25.1 and 26.2.

41 "According to the order of natural inclinations, therefore, is the order of precepts of the natural law. . . . and in keeping with this inclination those things that conserve human life (vita hominis) are in the field of natural law." *S.T.*, I-II, 94.2, Pegis ed., II, pp. 774-775. See Dom Odon Lottin, O.S.B., *Le Droit Natural chez Saint Thomas et sés prédécesseurs*, 2nd rev. ed., (Bruges: Beyaert, 1931), pp. 62-63.

42 See *S.T.*, I-II, 17.8.

43 ". . . et contra caritatem qua quilibet debet seipsum diligere."

44 ". . . quia naturaliter quaelibet res seipsum amat."

45 See *S.T.*, II-II, 23.6.

46 *Ibid.*, 23.1 Domin. ed. IX, pp. 263-264. See 24.2.

47 *Ibid.*, 26.4 Domin. ed. IX, p. 337.

48 "Murder is a sin, not only because it is contrary to justice, but also because it is opposed to charity which a man should have toward himself: in this respect suicide is a sin in relation to oneself." Domin. ed. X, p. 204.

49 However, more secularly oriented authors actually ignore the point about charity which Aquinas lays such stress on. See, e.g., Richard O'Sullivan, "The Ethics of Suicide: Aquinas and the Common Law," *The Catholic Lawyer*, II (1956), pp. 147-148.

50 ". . . the theological virtues direct man to supernatural happiness in the same way as by the natural inclination man is directed to his connatural end. . . . For the appetite of a thing is moved and tends towards its connatural end naturally; and this movement is due to a certain conformity of the thing with its end." *S.T.* I-II, 62.3, Pegis ed., II, p. 478. Note also: "These two principles i.e. love of God and man are the first common principles of the natural law and are self-evident to

human reason, either through nature or through faith." *Ibid.,* 100.3 ad 1, Pegis ed. II, p. 831.

[51] *In Libros Ethicorum,* Book VII, lesson 13, Leitzinger trans., II, p. 689: "Omnia habent in seipsis quoddam divinum, scilicet inclinationem naturae . . . hujus inclinationis principium."

[52] "The good we receive from God is twofold, the good of nature, and the good of grace. Now the fellowship of natural goods bestowed on us by God is the foundation of natural love . . . Wherefore much more is this realized with regard to the friendship of charity which is based on the fellowship of the gifts of grace." *S.T.* II-II, 26.3, Domin. ed., vol. IX, p. 335; cf. I, 62.2. See Joseph Buckley, S. M., *Man's Last End* (St. Louis and London: B. Herder, 1949), p. 178; W. B. Monahan, *The Moral Theology of St. Thomas Aquinas* I (London: E. Baylis and Son, 1942), p. 275.

[53] *S.T.* II-II, 23.2 Domin. ed. vol. IX, pp. 266-267. See John E. Naus, S.J., *The Nature of the Practical Intellect According to St. Thomas Aquinas* (Rome: Gregorian University, 1959), p. 29.

[54] See *S.T.* I-II, 85.1 and 2.

[55] See *S.T.* I-II, 94.2 Cf. 1,2.1. To persist in being is both a real (i.e., natural inclination) and an apparent (i.e., self-love) good. "By the apparent good, we mean that which is *called* 'good' by an individual because, and only because, it is in fact desired by him. . . . By the real good, we mean that which is good for an individual whether or not he is aware of desiring it; if he feels a desire for it, then the real good is also an apparent good for him; but if he does not, it still remains a real good for him." Adler, *The Time of Our Lives,* pp. 92-93.

[56] "Sed transitus de hac vita ad aliam feliciorem non subiacet libero arbitrio hominis, sed potestati divinae."

[57] See W. Farrell, O.P., *A Companion to the Summa* III (New York: Sheed and Ward, 1940), pp. 198-199; also Y. R. Simon, *Philosophy of Democratic Government,* p. 203.

[58] See Augustine *De Civitate Dei,* I. 20.

[59] *Ibid.,* I.25, trans. G. E. McCracken, vol. I, Loeb Classical Library (Cambridge, Mass.: Harvard University Press, 1957), pp. 107-109.

[60] "Fortitude" is the literal translation of *fortitudo;* however, "courage" better connotes this meaning in our contemporary usage.

[61] *S.T.,* II-II, 123.1 Domin. ed. XII, pp. 194-195. See a.3.

[62] *Ibid.,* I-II, 90.1; 91.3.

[63] See *S.T.,* II-II, 123.12.

[64] "But the dangers of death arising out of sickness, storms at sea, attacks from robbers, and the like, do not seem to come on a man through his pursuing some good. On the other hand, the dangers of death which occur in battle come to man directly on account of some good." *S.T.,* II-II, 123.5, Domin. ed. XII, p. 202.

[65] See *S.T.,* II-II, 64.6 ad 2.

[66] See Armstrong, *Primary and Secondary Precepts in Thomistic Natural Law Teaching,* pp. 110-111.

[67] See *S.T., II-II,* 58.5.

[68] "Cette fermeté qui résiste à l'instinct vital prend quelquefois une grandeur tragique. Mais il s'agit alors de courage psychologique, de courage nerveaux, si l'on peut ainsi dire, nonde courage moral. Le courage moral, qui est la vrai, puisque c'est celui de l'homme en tant qu'homme, consist dans la resistance à toute impulsion opposee au devoir." A. P. Sertillanges, *La Philosophie Morale de Saint Thomas d'Aquin,* rev. ed., (Paris: Aubier, 1946), p. 183.

69 *De Civitate Dei,* I.27, Loeb ed. vol. I, pp. 116-119. See D. Novak, *Law and Theology in Judaism* (New York: KTAV, 1974), pp. 84-86.

70 See *De Librio Arbitrio* V.11-VI.14; *De Trinitate* IX.6 for the priority of intrinsic over extrinsic considerations in Augustinian thought.

71 See *S.T.,* III, 47.6 ad 3.

72 *Nicomachean Ethics* 1128a5 ff., ed. H. Rackham, Loeb Classical Library (Cambridge, Mass.: Harvard University Press, 1926), pp. 318-321. The Greek text in Aristotle (p. 318) is unclear. Does he hold that suicide is a crime against natural law or only against the specific statute of the state? Aristotle's meaning here is vague as it is in other discussions in the *Nicomachean Ethics* on this point. See, e.g. 1134b20-1135a4.

73 "The Ethics of Suicide," pp. 177-178.

74 *S.T.* I-II, 96.4, Pegis ed. II, p. 795. Cf. II-II, 64.2.

75 See *S.T.,* II-II, 58.5.

76 ". . . this or that man may be considered as belonging to the State as part thereof, or as belonging to God, as His creature and image; and thus a man who kills himself, does an injury not indeed to himself, but to the State and to God." *S.T.,* II-II, 59.3 ad 2, Domin. ed. X., p. 141. Cf. *In Libros Ethicorum,* Book V, lesson 17.

77 See *Suicide,* trans. J. J. Spaulding and George Simpson, (Glencoe, Ill.: The Free Press, 1951), pp. 217-240.

78 See note 72.

79 *In Libros Ethicorum,* Book V, lesson 17, Litzinger trans. I, pp. 473-474: "et ita videtur guod occidere seipsum sit *per se injustum,* cum hoc lex nunquam praecipiat." Note also: "Unde manifestum est quod *ius est obiectum institiae." S.T.,* II-II, 57.1; Cf. 58.6. Aquinas' *ius* corresponds to Aristotle's *nomos.* For justice's status as the chief virtue see *S.T.,* I-II, 66.4.

80 *S.T.,* I-II, 95.2 Domin. ed. II, p. 784. Cf. "Since, then, the eternal law is the plan in the Chief Governor, all the plans of government in the inferior governors must be derived from the eternal law . . . Therefore, all laws, in so far as they partake of right reason, are derived from the eternal law." *S.T.,* I-II, 93.3, Pegis ed. II, p. 766.

81 ". . . man receives help from the group of which he is a part, to have a perfect sufficiency for life; namely that man may not only live but live well, having everything sufficient for living; . . ." *In Libros Ethicorum,* Book I, lesson 1, Litzinger trans. I, p. 7; Cf. Book, X, lesson 6.

82 Aristotle seems to disassociate himself from the Platonic notion which ascribed actual justice to the relationship of the parts of the soul to each other. "In a metaphorical and analogical sense, however, there is such a thing as justice, not towards oneself but between different parts of one's nature; not, it is true, justice in the full sense of the term but . . . a sort of justice . . ." *Nicomachean Ethics* 1138b5-10, Loeb ed., pp. 320-323. Aquinas refers to it, *In Libros Ethicorum,* Book V, lesson 17, as *similtudinarum iustum.* In the response to the first objection in the articel under discussion he writes: "non solum quia contrariatur justitiae."

83 See Jacques Maritain, *The Person and the Common Good,* trans. J. J. Fitzgerald (New York: Chas. Scribner's Sons, 1947), pp. 80 ff.; John Courtney Murray, *We Hold These Truths* (New York: Sheed and Ward, 1960), pp. 302 ff.

84 "The human will can, by common agreement, make a thing to be just provided it be not, of itself, contrary to natural justice . . . If, however, a thing is, of itself, contrary to natural right, the human will cannot make it just . . ." *S.T.,* II-II, 57.1 ad 2, Domin. ed. X, p. 105. See Adler, *The Time of Our Lives,* p. 140.

85 *S.T.,* II-II, 61.1, Domin. ed. X, pp. 158-159. Note: "In animal society, the *individual* is not a person; hence has not the value of a moral 'whole' and is not a subject of right. If the good of the whole profits the parts, as the good of the body profits its members, it does not in the sense that it is turned back or *redistributed* to them. It is merely in order that the whole itself might subsist and be better served that its parts are kept alive or maintained in good condition." Maritain, *The Person and the Common Good,* p. 39, n.28.

86 See Maritain, *op. cit.,* p. 39; and *S.T.,* I, 81.3.

87 Moreover, since every part is ordained to the whole as the imperfect to the perfect, and since one man is a part of the perfect community. Law must needs concern itself properly with the order directed to universal happiness. Therefore... the Philosopher mentions both happiness and the body politic..." *S.T.,* I-II, 90.2, Pegis ed. II, pp. 744-745. Cf. *Summa Contra Gentiles,* III, 112-113; Jacques Maritain, *Man and the State* (Chicago: University of Chicago Press, 1951), pp. 3 ff.

88 See Hook, "The Ethics of Suicide," p. 188. Cf. Durkheim, *Suicide,* pp. 152-216.

89 *In Libros Ethicorum,* Book I, lesson 2, Litzinger trans. I, p. 15: "Decitur autem hoc esse divinius eo quod magis pertinet ad Dei similitudinem, qui est ultima cause omnium bonorum."

90 See *De Civitate Dei,* XIV.1; Cf. Acts 5:30.

91 *S.T.,* I-II, 21.4 ad 3, Pegis ed. II, p. 365. Cf. 113.9 ad 2; II-II, 104.5.

92 "The human person is ordained directly to God as to its absolute ultimate end. Its direct ordination to God transcends every created common good—both the common good of the political society and the intrinsic common good of the universe... St. Thomas Aquinas, following the precedent set by Albert the Great, did not take over the doctrine of Aristotle without correcting and transfiguring it." Maritain, *The Person and the Common Good,* p. 5. See Bourke, *St. Thomas and the Greek Moralists,* p. 27.

93 Concerning Aquinas' political vocabulary which he uses in these discussions of the social realm, see Maritain, *Man and the State,* p. 30.

94 Aquinas justifies capital punishment on the grounds of social self-defense (see *S.T.,* II-II, 64.2). However, capital punishment is a derived precept which may be changed. See Thiry, "The Ethical Theory of Saint Thomas," pp. 175-176. For Aquinas' own reservations about capital punishment see *S.T.,* II-II, 64.6. Also, note in the very response under analysis: "ad solum enim Deum pertinet iudicium mortis et vitae."

95 "Nullus autem est index sui ipsius... Licet tamen ei se commitere iudicio aliorum."

96 "Tum etiam quia malefactorem occidere non licet nisi per iudicium publicae potestatis."

97 For the necessity of authority according to Thomistic social philosophy, see Gilson, *Moral Values and the Moral Life,* pp. 194-195 and the brilliant delineation of law and authority by Yves R. Simon, *A General Theory of Authority* (South Bend: University of Notre Dame Press, 1962), p. 48, n.11

98 See Simon, *op. cit.,* pp. 48-50.

99 *S.T.,* I-II, 90.4, Pegis ed. II, p. 746.

100 "In the opening chapter of the treatise *On The Governance of Rulers,* Aquinas leaves aside all substitutional and perfective functions of authority and delivers a straight exposition of its essential functions..." Simon, *Philosophy of Democratic Government,* p. 61, n.23.

101 See *S.T.,* I-II, 96.4; Cf. 92.1.

[102] "... it is lawful to kill an evildoer in so far as it is directed to the welfare of the whole community, so that it belongs to him alone who has charge of the community's welfare." *S.T.,* II-II, 63.3, Domin. ed. X, p. 200.

[103] "... vita est quoddam donum divinitus homini attributum, et eius potestati subiectum ... et sicut peccat ille qui usurput sibi iudicium de re sibi non commissa. Cf. ad 2: Nullus autem est index sui ipsius."

[104] E.g., see *S.T.,* I, 8.1 and 45.5. These and other similar references dealing with God's causality are given in the Caramello ed. II, p. 317.

[105] *S.T.,* I, 2.3.

[106] See *S.T.,* II-II, 59.3 ad 2.

[107] This approach is not exclusively Christian. Note: "The Romans found Rabbi Hanina ben Tradyon guilty of being absorbed in God's law and preaching to great assemblages. They wrapped him in the scroll he was using, bound him, and burned him at the stake. His students said to him, 'Rabbi, open your mouth and let the fire more quickly consume you.' He answered them, 'it is better that He who gave life should take it back; and let not a man destroy himself.'" Babylonian Talmud, *Tractate Abodah Zarah,* Romm ed. (Vilna, 1898), folio 18a [My translation].

[108] See Etienne Gilson, *Le Thomisme,* 5th ed., (Paris: J. Vrin, 1947), p. 434, where he writes: "Ce qu' Aristotle ne dit pas, et qui est beaucoup plus important, C'est que le suicide est une injustice à l'égard de Dieu." See also Gilson, *Moral Values and the Moral Life,* pp. 257-258.

[109] See *S.T.,* I-II, 100.5; and *De Regimine Principium,* Chap. XII; and H. V. Jaffa, *Thomism und Aristotelianism* (Chicago: University of Chicago Press, 1952), p. 169.

[110] "... ad hanc vitam, quae hominis libero arbitrio regitur."

[111] See *Summa contra Gentiles,* III, 112.

[112] See *S.T.,* II-II, 64.6.

[113] "Et ideo non licet homini seipsum interficere ut ad feliciorem transeat vitam. Similiter etiam nec miserias quaslibet huius sentis vitae evadat."

[114] See *S.T.,* I, 75.2 and 6.

[115] See *Summa Contra Gentiles,* III, 37-40, 48, 63.

[116] *S.T.* I, 82.3, Pegis ed. I, p. 780.

[117] See *S.T.* I, 82.4.

[118] "Our natural knowledge begins from sense. Hence our natural knowledge can go as far as it can be led by sensible things. But our intellect cannot be led by sense so far as to see the essence of God; because sensible creatures are effects of God, their cause. Hence from the knowledge of sensible things the whole power of God cannot be known; nor therefore can His essence be seen. But because they are His effects and depend on their cause, we can be led from them so far as to know of God *whether He exists*..." *S.T.* I, 12.12, Pegis ed. I, p. 109.

[119] See *Summa Contra Gentiles,* III, 40.

[120] See *S.T.,* I-II, 109.5; and 114.2. Cf. 73.9 ad 2.

[121] Aristotle, *Nicomachean Ethics* 1115a26-27, Loeb ed., pp. 154-155. Note: "The reason is that death is the end of all *present* life ... Things belonging to the state of the soul after death are not visible to us ..." Aquinas, *In Libros Ethicorum,* Book III, lesson 14, Litzinger trans. I, p. 236.

[122] "In weighing the gravity of a sin we must consider the essential rather than the accidental ... On the other hand, it is accidental to the slaying that the just man whose life is taken be received by God into glory." *S.T.* II-II, 64.6 ad 2, Domin. ed. V, p. 207.

[123] Augustine cautions: "Let anyone, therefore, who is told that he has no right to kill himself, do the deed if he is so ordered by him whose orders must not be slighted. There is just one proviso: he must be sure that his divine command is not made precarious by any doubt." *De Civitate Dei* I.26, Loeb ed. I, pp. 111-113. See *S.T.* II-II, 124.1, obj. 2 and reply *ad locum*.

[124] See *Commentary on the Ten Precepts*, no. 5; *Commentary to the Epistle to the Hebrews*, chap. 11, L. 7; *Commentary on the Sentences of Peter Lombard*, IV, 49, Q.5, a. 3, 9.2 ad 6.

[125] *La Philosophie Morale de Saint Thomas d'Aquin*, p. 183.

[126] See *Summa Contra Gentiles*, III, 99, 102.

[127] It is an especially vexing problem for Thomists. See Jacques Maritain, *Existence and the Existent*, trans. Lewis Galantiere and G. B. Phelan, Image Books (Garden City, N. Y.: Doubleday, 1957), pp. 65-67, where Maritain attempts to explain Abraham's willingness to sacrifice his son as a moral act, in contradistinction to Kierkegaard's "teleological suspension of the ethical."

CHAPTER IV

SUICIDE AND HUMAN PERSONALITY IN KANT

1. *Introduction.*

Suicide was surely an important philosophical problem for Kant, considering the number of times he discussed it. In four major ethical works we find six discussions of suicide. The earliest one is found in the *Lectures on Ethics,* a precritical work.[1] In the *Fundamental Principles of the Metaphysic of Morals* there are two discussions.[2] In the Critique of Practical Reason there are also two discussions.[3] Finally, there is the most specific discussion of suicide as a moral problem in the *Metaphysic of Morals.*[4] Because Kant discussed suicide so extensively, my first task is to determine the order in which the respective texts are to be examined.

The methodology of this chapter assumes that Kant's position on suicide grew, that is, in each subsequent discussion some new points are brought out. Hence the examination will proceed in the following order. Initially the first and second arguments in the *Fundamental Principles* will be analyzed along with the first and second arguments in the second *Critique.* Finally, the last and most specific treatment of the problem in the *Metaphysic* will be explicated.[5] The text in the *Lectures* will be regarded as a foreshadowing of the treatment of suicide in the critical philosophy, namely, a primitive expression of certain points more systematically developed later.[6] It will be brought in primarily as background.

2. *Fundamental Principles of the Metaphysics of Morals.*

After having set forth the first two formulations of the categorical imperative, namely, that a maxim must be capable of being conceived of as a universal law of nature, Kant proceeds to demonstrate just how duty is prescribed in some specific cases.

His first example is suicide. This is significant in that suicide involves the moral subject with an object more intimately experienced than any other, in an act involving the most fundamental condition of morality, life. With this in mind we can see why Kant takes suicide as the first moral problem for the application of the categorical imperative. If this problem cannot be solved, then it is difficult to see how any subsequent problems, involving less intimately experienced objects and less fundamental conditions, can be solved.

For Kant, the categorical imperative is the formulation of an a priori criterion for determining the morality of any practical maxim which might be proposed.[7] Certainly in the *Fundamental Principles,* ethics are rooted in the constitution of the individual person.[8] Therefore, if suicide is an everpresent possibility for the autonomous moral subject, then it is a problem of immediate significance for the moral theorist, who must begin with the specific problems of the moral subject.[9] For Kant the individual is that moral subject.[10] It is thus no accident that Kant, the moral theorist, chooses in both the *Fundamental Principles* and the second part of the *Metaphysic* to begin his discussion of specific moral problems with the question of suicide.

Now that we have seen the significance of the order of Kant's presentation of moral problems, let us proceed to the actual content of what he has to say about suicide. The first argument is as follows:

> A man reduced to despair by a series of misfortunes feels wearied of life, but is still so far in possession of his reason that he can ask himself whether it would not be contrary to his duty to himself to take his own life . . . His maxim is: From self-love I adopt it as a principle to shorten my life when its longer duration is likely to bring more evil than satisfaction. It is asked simply whether this principle founded on self-love can become a universal law of nature. Now we see at once that a system of nature of which it should be a law to destroy life by means of the very feeling whose special nature it is to impel to the improvement of life would contradict itself, and therefore could not exist as a system of nature; hence that maxim cannot possibly exist as a universal law of nature . . .[11]

This then is Kant's initial argument based upon the criterion of universalizability. The question is: How cogent is the argument? Is it a valid application of the categorical imperative? These questions have been posed

by a number of contemporary philosophers with whom I will deal shortly.
Let us examine these critical responses in order to bring to light the fuller
implications of the argument itself.

The point in the argument which most of Kant's critics have attacked
is his assumption that self-love is the cause of self-preservation, and that it
is a contradiction to posit self-love as the cause of self-destruction. Thus
even such a sympathetic commentator as H. J. Patton writes:

> In its strictest sense Kant takes a law of nature to be a causal
> law, and it is essential to such a law that it should have no excep-
> tions: the same cause must always produce the same effects . . . In
> the case of suicide, when Kant says that the 'determination' (*Bestim-
> mung*) of self-love is the furtherance of life, he means that this is its
> purpose or function and not merely its effect. . . . Why should it not be
> a merciful dispensation of Providence that the same instinct which
> ordinarily leads to life might lead to death when life itself offered
> nothing but continuous pain? This is the weakest of Kant's argu-
> ments.[12]

In other words, Paton has questioned the universalizability of Kant's
major premise, namely, it cannot be asserted as true that self-love entails
self-preservation in every case. Indeed, in some cases it would just as
easily seem to entail the opposite, suicide.

Following Paton another critic asserts that Kant has mistakenly assumed that self-love and self-preservation are in effect identical when
actually they are different. Self-preservation is an unconscious drive;
self-love is a drive both conscious and controllable by volition.[13] Thus
the connection between self-love and self-preservation is contingent on
circumstances.

Sir David Ross accuses Kant of describing a formal self-contradiction
which simply does not exist in fact. For him, self-love is the desire to get
pleasure and avoid pain; and life is at times pleasant and at other times
painful. In the latter case self-love would call for suicide.[14]

Thus all of these critics believe that Kant has made a moral judgment
contingent on a certain state of affairs. If so, then by Kant's own principles
such a judgment is not categorical but hypothetical. For Kant only categorical imperatives are moral. Hypothetical imperatives based on sensual
calculations are at best prudential but are not in themselves moral.[15]

Hence it would seem that these philosophers are attacking Kant for

making an empirical judgment which identifies self-love and self-preservation. All of them show how this judgment is easily falsified. They are thus
questioning Kant's judgment of the very data he presents. They are criticiz-
ing the sufficiency of Kant's argument based on the nature of self-love.[16]
There seems to be no reason why self-love cannot have two opposite
effects depending on one's circumstances: if good (that is pleasant) then
self-love ought to entail self-preservation; if bad (that is painful) then it
ought to entail self-destruction.

Nevertheless, these critics have failed to analyze what is implied by
the morally significant relation Kant posits between self-love and self-
preservation. None of them attempts to understand why for Kant a cause
can have only one effect in a morally constituted system of nature. They
have all assumed that Kant's argument is grounded in the specific nature
of self-love, and that self-preservation ought always to follow. Thus it has
been assumed that Kant is presenting a casual argument in the mode of
efficient casuality.

However, what they have missed is that the *Natur,*[17] is not grounded
in self-love; if it were it would be empirically constituted and could not
therefore be the ground of an authentically moral act.[18] A moral system of
nature for Kant is a world that follows from man's rational nature. It is
not the world of appearances in which man finds himself.[19] Self-love is
not the foundation of the *Natur* but is rather a *Bestimmung,* that is, a
"condition." [20] Thus self-love is subordinate to self-preservation as a
means to an end.[21] Self-preservation then is not merely *a* result of self-
love, it is *the end* of self-love.[22]

Apparently for Kant, an act of efficient casuality can have many possible results, but it can have only one authentic end.[23] Self-preservation
determines the constitution of self-love, not vice-versa. M. J. Gregor
brings this out very well.

> According to a classical example of Kantian criticism . . .
> suicide is immoral because if everyone were to act on a maxim of
> suicide, the human race, and with it the maxim of suicide itself,
> would become extinct. But Kant's own derivation of duties shows
> clearly that he is not thinking of logical consistency as the criterion
> of moral action. The freedom from contradiction which he requires
> in a universalized maxim is rather, a teleological consistency between
> our maxim and our objective, rational ends . . . in acting on a maxim

of arbitrarily destroying our capacity for free or moral action, we are in contradiction with our objective end as free as moral agents, and so in contradiction with ourselves.[24]

If Kant had only been more careful in indicating the subordinate status of the words beginning with "by means of the very feeling (*durch Dieselbe Empfindung*)" he would have avoided much misunderstanding. This system of nature is not constituted by efficient casuality, for efficient causes are themselves conditioned. It must then be constituted by unconditional casuality.[25]

It must now be ascertained just what Kant means by *Natur* in order to understand more fully his argument about suicide. In the second Critique Kant clarifies the meaning of *Natur* in moral discourse. The criterion of whether one's action could be part of a system of nature is not based upon any system of nature we know from experience. Indeed we can see from our own experience that if one commits suicide the whole natural order is not going to crumble with him, anymore than private property will disappear if one person steals. However, such is the case because in the system of nature, empirically conceived, we are parts of a whole whose structural foundations lie outside of us. It is because of this empirical heteronomy that we cannot derive our morally constituted autonomy from nature.

On the other hand, every rational being must ideally constitute the moral system of nature for himself. The system of nature follows from the nature of the moral subject himself.[26] That is why it is autonomous, that is, a free creation of reason. Therefore, although it must apply to objects in the world of sense it is not grounded in any sensuous considerations. Thus Kant refers to the comparison of moral law with universal natural law as "a type for the estimation of maxims according to moral principles." [27]

Since morality is only authentic when constituted on autonomous grounds, when one contemplates suicide he cannot reason that the morally constituted natural order will go on without him. For since the universal law of nature is only a *type* for autonomous morality, there can be no universal moral order without the moral subject himself being present. He is its necessary and sufficient principle. This system of nature then is grounded in man, not man in the system of nature.[28] The system of nature is the possible outcome of human moral constitution of the world. It itself is ideal. But, in order for it to be intelligible, and not just imaginative, it must be grounded in something having real presence. In this way Kant distinguishes his idealism from that of Plato.[29]

It is only when we understand the fundamental difference between an empirical system of nature of which man is but one part, and a moral system of nature of which man is the foundation, that we can understand the following argument Kant presents in the second *Critique*.

> Also the maxim which I adopt in respect to freely disposing of my life is at once determined when I inquire what it would have to be in order that a system of nature could maintain itself in accordance with such a law. Obviously in such a system of nature no one could arbitrarily end his life, for such an arrangement could not constitute a permanent natural order.[30]

In an empirical system of nature the above argument would obviously be absurd. People commit suicide every day and the world goes on. However, this is because the system of nature of which these people are part is not grounded in them. They are not necessary for its permanence, rather they are contingent in relation to it.

Yet this is so because the empirical order of nature is sensuously, not rationally, constituted. Were it rationally constituted by an autonomous being, then the system itself would be contingent on the presence of that being. This is what Kant is saying. The natural order the person constitutes when he applies the categorical imperative is contingent on the individual moral subject; he constitutes it by himself. It is ideal not real.[31] Therefore, its permanence presupposes his presence. For Kant the moral order is wholly anthropocentric in that it centers around the individual person as the moral subject.

Morality reconstitutes the two orders in which the person as a sensuous being participates, namely, nature and society. Nature, morally considered, now becomes a type of estimation for the moral law, that is, a model for universalizability.[32] Society, morally considered, becomes, on the other hand, the "realm of ends," namely, the ideal communion of free and rational moral beings. Both nature and society presuppose the human person as *causa noumenon*,[33] that is a cause which is irreducible, intelligent and free. Suicide is immoral because by it one removes himself from these two ideal orders of which he is the foundation. Therefore, morally speaking, they cannot endure or even be considered without him.

Thus in the second critique Kant states:

> If one belonged to such an order of things that anyone . . . felt
> justified in shortening his life as soon as he was thoroughly wearly
> of it . . . would be assent of his own will to being a member of such
> an order of things? [34]

If we compare the two arguments in the second *Critique* we can see that neither one makes sense if we regard the person as simply a part of an order whose foundation is independent of his own free and rational agency. Obviously, if one can choose whether or not to be part of such an order his participation does not imply any heteronomy, that is, he is in no way contingent on this order. In the empirical order of nature one has no such choice. Empirically speaking, even the act of suicide does not remove one from the natural order, because the very efficient casuality involved in suicide is still subject to natural law. The law of the sequential order of cause and effect still applies.[35]

In his third formulation of the categorical imperative in the *Fundamental Principles,* namely, that acts are only moral in that they treat their human objects as ends in themselves, Kant again uses suicide as his first example. Each formulation of the categorical imperative is meant to be a conclusive criterion for judging the morality of any act. This is why Kant repeats his cases, to show, for example, the equivalence of the various ways one can judge suicide to be immoral.

In terms of the categorical imperative itself, any of its formulations ought to suffice for the case at hand. However, in many cases one formulation is going to turn out to be a good deal more intelligible and convincing than another. In our specific case of suicide the third formulation seems to provide a more understandable prohibition of suicide than the earlier formulations. That Kant himself also thought this is indicated by his later treatment of suicide in the *Metaphysic.* There his argument is based on the third formulation. The issues raised in the first two formulations are not even taken up.

After stating his third formulation, Kant applies it to the case of suicide as follows.

> To abide by the previous examples: *First,* under the head of
> necessary duty to oneself: He who contemplates suicide should ask
> himself whether his action can be consistent with the idea of humanity

as an *end in itself*. If he destroys himself in order to escape from
painful circumstances, he uses a person merely as *a means* to maintain a tolerable condition up to the end of life. But a man is not a
thing, that is to say, something which can be used merely as a means,
but must in all his actions be always considered as an end in himself.[36]

This argument is a good deal more convincing than the first one.

Kant is saying that there are two kinds of ends, phenomenal and
noumenal. Phenomenal ends, such as the avoidance of pain or disgrace
are conditioned, that is, they can be reduced to the situation of the individual. They are, in short, the product of feeling. Noumenal ends, on the
other hand, are the only authentic ends in themselves, and they are by
definition irreducible. Anything which is reducible and which stands in
relation to an end which is irreducible assumes the status of a means.

The judgment to commit suicide relates means and ends in reverse
order. Self-love becomes the end, and the whole life of the moral subject,
who as a person is a *causa noumenon,* becomes the means to this end.
However, anything which contradicts life and which is grounded in any
sensuous considerations whatsoever is morally illegitimate.[37] In terms of
pure practical theory this illegitimacy is the result of substituting the reducible means for the irreducible end, the phenomenal aspect of the person
for the noumenal, the apparent for the real, the sensuous for the moral.
Herein lies the contradiction (*Widerspruch*). This conditional status of the
phenomenal aspect of human life to the noumenal aspect is later brought
out even more explicitly in the *Metaphysic*.[38]

Now, in order to understand Kant's second argument for the prohibition of suicide we must understand how he understands an end in itself
(*Zweck an sich selbst*).

It would seem at first glance that Kant's identification of end and
moral casuality might place him in the philosophical tradition of natural
law, where morality is constituted on the basis of teleology. By determining the irreducible ends which man encounters in his practical experience
we are able to determine the primary precepts of natural law. Because
human experience is varied and complex, various ends are discovered;
there is not just one primary precept of natural law, although there is a
first principle of practical reason, as I have discussed the theory in my
treatment of Aquinas. These goods in relation to our human inclinations
have a primary or original status. This notion of the role of ends involves
considerable breadth, for it recognizes a plurality of goods and it also

recognizes a distinction between the goods themselves and the moral subject who strives towards them.

However, whereas the philosophical tradition of natural law, especially as presented in the writings of Aquinas, attempted to develop this breadth, Kant, on the other hand, attempted to narrow the notion of end in morality. He attempted to do this in three steps. (1) He designated ends which are objects of sensuous experience as projections of the particular disposition of the individual. (2) He designated ends which are not objects of sensuous experience, but objects posited by unrestrained speculation, (especially, God and immortality) as postulates of pure practical reason. (3) By a process of elimination as it were we are left with the moral subject himself. This further constrained the notion of end by eliminating any distinction between the irreducible end sought and the moral subject who seeks it.

In the case of suicide we find the grounds for the prescription of its immorality not to be sensuous considerations of self-love, nor the postulatory considerations of God and immortality, but the sole ground becomes the irreducibility, or in practical language the inviolability, of the moral subject by any phenomenal consideration whatsoever. These successive reductions explain why for Kant there is only one ground for the prohibition of suicide, whereas for Aquinas there are three independent grounds for this prohibition, namely, natural inclination, sociality, and Divine lordship.

For Kant, an end to have moral force must be irreducible. At this point he is one with the philosophical tradition of natural law. It too posits the metaphysical priority of ends over means. However, although Kant's very choice of the term *Zweck* deliberately corresponds to the classical terms *telos* and *finis,* nevertheless he limits the moral value of *Zweck* to the moral subject himself. In other words, the task of Kant's moral teleology is not to develop new concepts as much as it is to redefine the old concepts coming from the long tradition of teleological reflection.

Therefore, it is important that we have a clear understanding of the teleology Kant is redefining in the *Fundamental Principles.* This redefinition involves a further reduction of what had theretofore been accepted as irreducible, for Kant is further developing the tradition of teleology in his own way. This is evident in Kant's use of three basic German terms for what in English we call *end.* By differentiating their respective meanings he is able to accomplish the limitation of end that he wishes to accomplish, that is, he is able to show that only one meaning of the term end is truly irreducible.

The first term is *Ende* in the sense of a temporal completion. Thus in
the second argument in the *Fundamental Principles* against suicide Kant
writes: "If he destroys himself in order to escape painful circumstances he
uses a person as *a means* to maintain a tolerable condition up to the end
of life (bis zu Ende des Lebens)." [39] This use of *end* corresponds to the
early Greek meaning of *telos,* a meaning later signified by the word
eschaton.[40] However, this meaning of the term end was precluded from
being a standard of moral judgment by Aristotle in his treatment of
"Solon's Paradox" in the first book of the *Nicomachean Ethics,*[41] because
the only meaning of end which is practically significant is when an end is
an intelligible goal for human action in the present. For this reason
Aristotle limits the moral significance of the term *telos* to that of *intelligible
purpose.* I know of no other philosopher between Aristotle and Kant who
attempted to override Aristotle on this point.[42] It is important to realize that
because of the tradition of teleological reflection Kant did not have to
bother with eliminating *Ende* as a moral ground. No one held otherwise.

The second modality of end which he excludes as a standard for moral
reasoning is *Absicht.*[43] Early in the *Fundamental Principles* Kant states:
". . . an action done from duty (*Pflicht*) derives its moral worth (*Wert*),
not from the purpose (Absicht) which is to be attained by it, but from the
maximum by which it is determined . . ." [44] In the following paragraph
Kant sees *Absicht* as grounded in "inclination" (*Neigung*) and *Pflicht* as
grounded in "respect" (*Achtung*). From this we see that *Absicht* which
is loosely translated as "purpose" is the result of inclination. Inclination
may agree with morality to be sure, but inclination does not itself constitute a standard for moral judgment because it is not irreducible.[45]

Earlier Kant illustrates this point with the very example of the duty
to preserve one's life:

> . . . it is a duty to maintain one's life; and, in addition, everyone has
> also a direct inclination to do so. But on this account the often
> anxious care which most men take for it has no intrinsic worth, and
> their maxim has no moral import. They preserve their life *as duty
> requires,* no doubt, but not *because duty requires.* On the other
> hand, if adversity and hopeless sorrow have completely taken away
> the relish for life, if the unfortunate one, strong in mind, indignant at
> his fate rather than desponding or dejected, wishes for death, and yet
> preserves his life without loving it—not from inclination or fear, but
> from duty—then his maxim has a moral worth.[46]

What Kant has done is to contrast two motives for action. Action motivated by duty is essentially moral; action motivated by inclination is not essentially moral, and if it is in conflict with duty it is immoral. Duty for duty's sake is to be understood as moral action for the sole sake of the moral end.[47] *Neigung* is for Kant *inclinatio*.

In the previous chapter we saw how Aquinas grounded the prohibition of suicide in the fact that it is contrary to natural inclination. If self-preservation were taken as an end because it is a natural inclination, then, for Kant, it would be as sensuously constituted as self-love, and could no more than self-love be the irreducible ground for a morally constituted system of nature. The person as an end in himself is a noumenon; natural inclination is a phenomenon. Therefore, authentic duty, which is noumenally grounded, cannot be grounded in inclination.

Kant rejects *Neigung* as a ground for moral judgment because it is reducible to pathological feelings. As such they are empirical facts only which are not on the level of conceptual judgments, much less on the level of the intelligible casuality of moral ideas. They are neither necessary nor universal. These pathological feelings are for Kant, the most contingent and enigmatic factors in human experience. They have no stability and they are dangerous if not controlled by factors more stable and more intelligible. Feelings are on the lowest level of *Sinnlichkeit*. Kant is continually contemptuous of any attempt to base human action on feelings. Therefore, he rejects *Neigung* as a moral ground.[48]

As one commentator notes about Kant's position on this notion:

> "The usage of Neigung to refer to settled disposition is not always observed. It generally means any inclination and is approximately equivalent to *Triebfeder* except when *Triebfeder* refers to the moral incentive or motive."[49]

To act on the basis of inclination is to act from desire, which is the link between feelings and actions. Consequently the rule of desire, prudence, becomes "cleverness" (Klugheit).[50] Its status as the virtue of *prudentia* is removed by Kant. In the case of suicide the natural inclination to preserve life is wholly unreliable because it has no more priority for prudential judgment than "death wishes;" both are in essence feelings. The very contingency of feelings makes one no more necessary than the other. On the level of inclination one either feels like living or one does not; how he happens to feel is his inclination.

Of course this identification of inclination with a state of feeling is probably what most people would today assume. To say, "I am not inclined to preserve my life," and to say, "I do not feel like living," is to say the same thing in our ordinary language.[51] However, this equation was not always made. As we saw in the last chapter, the notion of *inclinatio naturalis* is rooted in teleology. Thus the inclination to preserve life, being grounded in a real good—life, persists even in particular situations where one's feelings are not in accord with it. The moral choice is to choose the specific inclination over the particular feeling. Every act has its own proper end which is prior to it. As such, the ends of human inclination are more than subjective purposes which can be reduced to the emotional state of the individual person.

However, if teleology is only meaningful in describing human action but not human nature as is the case for Kant, then all ends become subsequent to human action and thereby lose whatever priority they would otherwise have. With the loss of this priority they cannot very well be standards for the moral judgment of human actions. There are no real and irreducible moral ends outside of man himself considered as a rational person, as a *causa noumenon*. There are no unconditional goods in the world outside of the autonomous moral subject. Considerations of natural teleology do not even enter the primary intuitions of time and space nor the tables of categories and judgments. As such, there are no teleological schemata connecting intuition with judgment.[52] For Kant all objects of desire are human projects (*Absicht*). As such, they cannot be standards of moral judgment.

With this development in mind, one can appreciate that Kant's contempt for *Neigung* as the ground for the prohibition of suicide is not just an intellectual's disdain for an emotional approach to human problems, but is a philosophical reworking of the notion of end, a notion which played such a crucial role in the previous history of moral discourse. Instead of morality presupposing teleology Kant reverses the relation; now teleology can only be understood subsequent to morality. Its function is now symbolic.[53]

Just as Kant made sensuous purposiveness a human project, and, therefore, destroyed whatever priority it had over the situation of the particular individual, so Kant made God a postulate of pure practical reason. Just as Kant removed natural inclination from consideration as an independent ground of morality by making its value depend on something else, so did Kant, as early as the *Lectures,* make God subsequent as well.

> But as soon as we examine suicide from the standpoint of religion we immediately see it in its true light. We have been placed in this world under certain conditions and for specific purposes' (*Absichten*). But a suicide opposes the purpose (*Zweck*) of his Creator, he arrives in the other world as one who has deserted his post; he must be looked upon as a rebel against God . . . But suicide is not inadmissable and abominable because God has forbidden it; God has forbidden it because it is abominable in that it degrades man's inner worth below that of animal creation.[54]

In the first half of the quoted passage, Kant has simply repeated the traditional argument of Plato and Aquinas concerning man as the subject of God, which means that the relationship with God constitutes an independent ground for the suicide prohibition. However, in the second half of the quote he states what by the time of the critical philosophy will become his own position. God himself is subsequent to a fully constituted rational morality. The lordship of God for Kant, can no longer be considered as an independent ground for morality. The *Lectures* are based on Baumgarten's *Ethica,* a standard textbook for university courses in ethics at that time.[55] They do not always reflect Kant's own position.

To see how the discussion in the *Lectures* about God's authority is a primitive expression of a theme later developed in the critical philosophy we need only look at the following passage from the first *Critique:* "So far, then, as practical reason has the right to serve as our guide, we shall not look upon actions as obligatory because they are the commands of God, but shall regard them as divine commands because we have an inward obligation to them."[56] If the respective German texts are examined one will immediately notice all the same key terms are used in both.

Thus, if natural inclination is beneath human nature and incapable of grounding rational morality, then God as an *ens noumenon* is too far beyond human grasp to be an intelligible ground for morality. Only God as conceived in a way postulatory to morality can be invoked in the prohibition of suicide. In this postulatory capacity it would be an outright contradiction to see God as an independent ground for the prohibition of suicide. It must be emphasized that for Kant we have no direct duties to God as is the case for both Plato and Aquinas.

This view is a radical departure from both Plato and Aquinas who argue that suicide is immoral because it usurps the authority of God as discovered by human reason. It is true that for both of them God cannot contradict rational morality. But in direct contradistinction to Kant, the authority of God is itself a rational ground, that is, we have direct duties to God our maker as we have direct duties to ourselves and other men.

By reducing inclinations to the level of *Absicht* and the idea of God to the level of a postulate,[57] Kant has identified the notion of end with man the rational being, the moral subject. That man is an end in himself is not original with Kant, for natural law theory certainly had previously emphasized the inviolability of the human person. Theology, too, emphasized man's status as the image of God.

But whereas the inviolability of man for natural law theory presupposed a natural order in which man participates, for Kant to regard man as *Zweck an sich selbst* is to regard man as uniquely and singularly the ground of all value.

All this was accomplished by a carefully and persuasively executed process of elimination. For Kant the only meaning of end having immediate moral value was *Zweck an sich selbst* which he made synonomous with man. Thus in the third *Critique* Kant writes:

> Now of man (and so every rational creature in the world) as a moral being it can no longer be asked why (quem in finem) he exists. His existence involves the highest purpose to which, as far as is in his power, he can subject the whole of nature . . . Only in man, and only in him as the subject of morality, do we meet with unconditioned legislation in respect of purposes, which therefore alone renders him capable of being a final purpose (Endzweck), to which the whole of nature is teleologically subordinated.[58]

Thus Kant has determined the exact locus of the human person. One is a person in that he is a moral being.[59] By so doing he has reconstituted morality, especially the traditional prohibition of suicide. Man is not part of a previously constituted moral system of nature, rather this system follows from his own nature in an apodictic way. Every rational person is the foundation of this system. The rationality of the system depends on the human person as its foundation. Kant thus explains the immediate interest we take in moral actions.[60] The human person alone confers moral value on the universe.

3. *Metaphysic.*

The main point of the discussion of suicide in the *Metaphysic* is that man as a moral being cannot be sacrificed for any sensuous purposes. This argument is a restatement of the second argument in the *Fundamental Principles,* namely, man must regard himself as an end in himself and hence ought not to sacrifice himself for any sensuous considerations whatsoever. Nevertheless, the discussion of suicide in the *Metaphysic* does contain two factors absent from the earlier treatments of suicide. The first is a criticism of the Stoic permission of suicide. The second factor is the five casusitical questions, that is, five cases in which suicide might be considered morally acceptable on the basis of a conflict between noumenal and phenomenal ends.

Stoicism was the one school of ancient philosophy that considered suicide a legitimate moral option. Kant could not very well ignore this position inasmuch as it might seem to rest upon premises similar to his own. In fact, the seeming similarity of Stoic morality to his own forced Kant in his ethical works to deal with Stoicism more extensively than any other school of moral philosophy. Concerning the Stoic position on the question of suicide Kant writes:

> It seems absurd that a man can injure himself (*volenti non fit injuria*). The Stoic therefore considered it a prerogative of his personality as a wise man to walk out of this life with an undisturbed mind whenever he liked (as out of a smoke-filled room), not because he was afflicted by actual or anticipated ills, but simply because he could make use of nothing more in this life.[61]

Kant's presentation of the Stoic permission of suicide bases it on the notion that man cannot really harm himself. This argument was first presented by Plato in the *Republic*.[62] There Plato argues that any action where the self is both subject and object is absurd if we regard the self as a simple undivided entity. Such a relation is ruled out by the law of non-contradiction. Therefore, the only intelligible understanding of reflexive action is one in which we understand the self to be a complex, divided entity, that is, we must posit an internal relation between the parts of the self. Even Aristotle, in his treatment of suicide, as we have seen, agrees with Plato in admitting this point concerning suicide as a crime against the self.[63]

Plato's example of "self-mastery" only has meaning when it is understood as the mastery of one part of the self by another. However, the very fact that a relation within the self is possible, and that it is one of mastery, indicates that this relation is not one of equal parts. Rather, it is between higher and lower parts. For Plato, the higher part of the self is the immortal soul and the lower part is the perishable body and its appetites. The immortal soul exerts mastery over the perishable body. The body cannot exert any real mastery over the soul. At most the body can become a distraction, diverting the soul from its proper end, contemplation. Therefore, the perishable body cannot destroy that which is immortal by nature.

With this understood, we can see how the Stoics concluded that suicide is a legitimate moral act. If the soul is the higher part of the self and the body is the lower part, then their relation is one of master-slave: the body's proper function is to serve the needs of the soul. Therefore, if the body and its sphere of operation are no longer of any use to the soul's rational end, then the soul seems to be perfectly justified in severing its connection with the body. Suicide for the Stoics is the soul's detachment from the cumbersome body. Cebes also argued against Socrates' prohibition of suicide in the *Phaedo* that the doctrine of the immortality of the soul implies that suicide is permissible.

Kant faced as formidable a challenge in Stoicism as Plato faced in Cebes. For Kant's understanding of the relation between *homo noumenon* and *homo phaenomenon* seems to correspond to the Platonic-Stoic understanding of the relation between the immortal soul and the perishable body. If the soul is immortal, then obviously suicide cannot be taken as self-destruction in an absolute sense. Furthermore, the Stoic maxim seems to be: The body exists as the servant of the soul. When it is helpful to the pursuits of the soul it ought to be kept in service. However,.when it is no longer needed it ought to be dismissed as one would dismiss a no longer useful servant. This would not be a maxim based on sensuous considerations of self-love, on pathological grounds. Rather, it seems to rest on an understanding of the relation between reason and sense quite similar to Kant's. Therefore, Kant must show why indeed he cannot accept the Stoic alternative; he must further develop his own position.

In answer to this challenge Kant writes:

And yet this very courage, this strength of mind—of not fearing death and of knowing of something which man can prize more highly than his life—ought to have been an ever so much greater motive for him not to destroy himself, a being having such authoritative superiority; consequently, it ought to have been a motive for him not to deprive himself of life.[64]

This answer requires considerable explication to be intelligible, much less convincing.

Kant attributes the Stoic motive to "courage" which he calls "strength of mind" (*Seelenstärke*). He argues that courage ought to inspire one to persist in life rather than terminate it. However, courage as *Seelenstärke* ought to indicate the soul's independence of the body. Therefore, suicide, which releases the soul from the chains of the body, ought to be considered pre-eminently courageous. Yet, Kant insists that courage demands that one refrain from suicide.[65]

Now, this insistence is indeed understandable when suicide is based on sensuous motives, for in that case the soul is as it were, doing the body's bidding. However, since the Stoic's motive is spiritual and not physical, why can his suicide not be justified by the virtue of courage? Is not his suicide a case of spiritual strength rather than of weakness? The answer to this vital question of interpretation depends on how we interpret the words: "not to destroy himself, a being having such authoritative superiority over the strongest sensible incentives." The question is: *Just who is destroying whom in the act of suicide?*

In defining suicide in this article Kant states: "The deliberate killing of oneself . . . can be called self-murder only when it can be shown that the killing is really a crime committed against one's own person . . ."[66] Later on he writes: "Accordingly, to dispose of oneself as a mere means to some end of one's own liking is to degrade the humanity in one's person (*homo noumemenon*), which, after all, was entrusted to man (*homo phaenomenon*) to preserve."[67] Therefore, the object of the act of suicide is the self as a person, a noumenon, and the subject of the act is the self as a *Mensch,* a phenomenon. Here is Kant's point of difference from the Stoics. Phenomenal man is considered to be the custodian of noumenal man. For Plato and the Stoics, on the other hand, the soul is the custodian of the body. This relationship of custody is set up by God. Thus Kant has posited the relationship of custody inversely. It is ironic, though, that he nevertheless retains the custodial analogy with its overtones of a meaning he has just reversed.[68]

Here we find the greatest difficulty in Kant's suicidology. If phenomenal man has custody of noumenal man, then we have a casual relation between them. But then noumenal man would be part of a casual order, a time sequence. However, how can Kant possibly maintain such a position inasmuch as the noumena are by definition beyond any phenomenal limitations? They limit phenomena; phenomena do not limit them.[69] This is surely a most serious paradox within Kant's ethical system.

This problem is difficult to solve. One could say, taking the path of least resistance, that the *Metaphysic* was written by Kant in his last years, and that it reflects his haste to complete his critical philosophy before he died. Thus its arguments are not as carefully or as extensively developed as those in his earlier, more youthful, works. Hence, one might charitably make certain concessions to the waning intellectual powers of an aged philosopher. However, the antinomy I have just suggested is so important that one might see it as a refutation of the practical applicability of Kant's ethical principles. Philosophers, whose ethical principles would conflict with Kant's rejection of natural inclination as a moral ground, could easily seize upon this antinomy and expand it into a general case against the practical applicability of Kantian ethics as a whole.

The antinomy cannot be completely solved, since any solution has to suppose what Kant himself might have answered had he lived to deal with the objection. Nevertheless, my exegesis of this section of the *Metaphysic* would not be complete if I did not attempt a plausible explanation. The following might clear up some of the problems.

Kant's sharp distinction between *homo noumenon* and *homo phaenomenon* seems to imply that he is talking about two separate entities in conflict with one another; each of them an independent center of consciousness and volition. However, phenomena cannot be regarded as conscious and volitional. Therefore, such an interpretation does not do justice to Kant's ethics which sees moral conflict as a struggle *within one person*.[70] Man, in this world, is one person with two orientations: a phenomenal orientation in which he responds to impulses caused by forces outside his will; and a noumenal orientation in which he acts as a free and intelligent cause. The phenomenal orientation is heteronomously constituted; the noumenal, autonomously constituted. In the case of a conflict between phenomenal desire and noumenal duty, morality demands the subordination of the former to the latter. This subordination consists of making the noumenal factor the ground of the act, the phenomenal factor the condition of the act. In other words, the phenomenal factor becomes the means, the noumenal the end. Hence, in the case of suicide, phenomenal self-love is the condition of the act of maintaining one's life; man as an end in himself (noumenon) is the ground of the act.

Therefore, if one makes an immoral decision, that is, has formulated an immoral maxim, he has eliminated the noumenal factor in favor of the phenomenal factor for the duration of the act. Thus, for example, if one decides to cheat some other person, he has eliminated for himself the noumenal status of that other person (as an end in himself) for the duration of the act of cheating. Likewise, as regards suicide, one has eliminated his own noumenal status for the duration of the act. Moreover, in the case of suicide, unlike cheating, we know of nothing beyond the duration of the act.[71] Its effect is permanent as far as our finite knowledge is concerned.

Therefore, it can be argued, on Kant's behalf, that suicide is not the actual murder of the noumenal man by the phenomenal; it is rather, the person's destruction of the possibility of any further relation between the phenomenal condition (life) and the noumenal ground (morality) of human action. Thus the one who commits suicide destroys the condition of morality. As Kant puts it:

> To destroy the subject of morality in his own person is tantamount to obliterating from the world, as far as he can, the very existence of morality itself . . .[72]

Here Kant states that suicide destroys the existence (Existenz) of morality for himself. Thus, for example, one can destroy his own existence as a being, but he cannot destroy the *essence,* humanity. It seems that Kant understands *existence* as the condition for the manifestation of a moral idea in the world. Suicide destroys the existential condition of morality, but not morality *in essence* which is an idea; ideas, being noumenal, are not subject to phenomenal causes.

Now we can understand Kant's refutation of the Stoic position. The refutation is based on Kant's refusal to accept immorality, that is, life after death, or *life after suicide* in this case, as an authentic moral ground. Immortality, like God, is a postulate of pure practical reason. That is its only legitimate function, for Kant. Hence the Stoic, acting on a spurious moral ground, is guilty of self-murder. He has destroyed his life, the existential condition of his moral personality.

For Kant, the immortality of the soul is a postulate of pure practical reason, that is, it is a theoretical requirement which must be entertained if our morality is to be thoroughly workable.[73] Nevertheless, it is a subsequent requirement of our moral reasoning, a corollary, and it cannot be taken as a ground of moral action. It has no status independent of or prior to morality. Therefore, one cannot draw any moral conclusions from the postulates of pure practical reason. They can only be invoked to further clarify action which has already been justified by the one ground of all moral action—the person as an end in himself. Any conclusions drawn from the three postulates of pure practical reason God, immortality, and freedom, which in any way contradict conclusions drawn from authentically moral grounds, are illegitimate.

We saw previously that the relationship with God is not an independent ground for the prohibition of suicide as it was for Plato and Aquinas. This is why Kant does not counter the Stoic permission of suicide, as Plato countered the objection of Cebes in the *Phaedo,* with arguments based on God's lordship. In like manner, one cannot draw any independent conclusions from the postulate of the immortality of the soul, for Kant specifically indicates that the postulate of the immortality of the soul is required by pure practical reason because the complete fitness of the will to the moral law can only be found in an endless progress, that is, in an infinitely enduring existence for the personality of the rational being.

The important point to remember is that we postulate immortality because of morality. Obviously, then, we cannot draw any independent conclusions from immortality. It itself is a corollary of morality. Suicide is immoral, as we have seen by using the second and third formulations of the categorical imperative. Hence we cannot take immortality as a legitimate moral ground for committing suicide, because postulates of pure practical reason can not be taken as grounds for morally acceptable acts, much less for morally unacceptable acts.

Furthermore, phenomenal considerations such as self-love are inadmissible as moral grounds and are actually immoral if they are used as reasons for acts which contradict the grounds of morality as formulated by the categorical imperative. Also, noumenal projections such as God and immortality are inadmissable as moral grounds, and they are actually immoral if they are used as reasons for acts which contradict the grounds of morality. Thus the Stoic attempt to ground the act of suicide in a consideration of immortality is just as immoral as the hedonist's attempt to ground the act of suicide in a consideration of self-love. Self-love, on the one hand, and immortality, on the other hand, are only morally legitimate when they are subordinated to the authentic grounds of morality; self-love as a means, immortality as a postulate.

Hence, when Kant speaks of "authoritative superiority over the strongest sensible incentives," he is referring to moral control over *both* phenomenal and noumenal excesses. This equation of the errors of hedonism and the errors of rationalism is clearly brought out in the second *Critique*.

> It is astonishing how otherwise acute men believe they can find a difference between the lower and the higher faculty of desire by noting whether the conceptions which are associated with pleasure have their origin in the senses or in the understanding . . . However dissimilar the conceptions of the objects, be they proper to the understanding or even to the reason instead of the senses, the feeling of pleasure by which they constitute the determining ground of the will (since it is the agreeableness and enjoyment which one expects from the object which impels the activity toward producing it) is always the same.[74]

Kant specifically identifies the error of hedonism, that is, the error of positing sensuous grounds for morality, with Epicureanism. Stoicism, on the other hand, is criticized for positing external (heteronomous) rational grounds for morality. The theoretical error of both is, however, the same, namely, their grounds are not autonomous.[75] This is why Kant refers to the authority of practical reason over sensuous incentives, that is, over all maxims grounded in considerations of pleasure, be that pleasure physical or spiritual.

To ground one's act in considerations of immortality is as morally fallacious as to ground one's act in considerations of sensuous self-love. Neither the sensuous nor the other rational consideration can morally justify suicide. The sensuous maxim has already been rejected by the arguments of the *Fundamental Principles* supplemented by the discussions in the second *Critique*. The rational maxim could not be taken up until a later period in the development of the critical philosophy. It is only intelligible *after* Kant's treatment of Stoic morality in the second *Critique*. In other words, it could not be taken up until additional distinctions between the Kantian position and the Stoic position had been brought out.

4. *Casuistical Questions.*

The casuistical questions which Kant raises at the end of each article in the Metaphysic comprise an important and little appreciated aspect of his moral philosophy. Unlike the *Fundamental Principles* and the second *Critique* which deal with specific moral problems only as illustrations of general principles, the *Metaphysic* primarily deals with the specific moral problems themselves and attempts to judge them in the light of the general moral principles Kant developed in his earlier works. Thus the treatment of these questions in the *Metaphysic* is more thorough; it deals with every aspect of the question itself.

This difference in approach clearly manifests itself in the treatment of suicide in the *Metaphysic*. For in the *Fundamental Principles* and the second *Critique* suicide is not dealt for itself, but is rather chosen as an example because of certain of its specifics which illustrate the general moral principles. However, the treatment of suicide in the *Metaphysic* begins with suicide itself, and then the appropriate moral principles are brought into play. Thus the point of difference lies in the respective subject matter under analysis. The *Metaphysic* is interested in an exhaustive analysis of suicide as a moral problem and in every possible maxim which could be proposed to justify it.

The casuistical questions deal with aspects of suicide which are difficult to relate to Kant's general moral principles.[76] They involve specific cases in which it is difficult to determine whether suicide would be moral or immoral. Obviously, they involve cases where an unambiguous moral judgment is impossible; otherwise Kant would surely have solved them as he did those cases in which the maxim is based on illegitimate considerations of either sense or reason. The casuistical questions concern those "loose ends" which cannot be related to Kant's moral principles by any straight line of argument. Kant refers to them as "exercises."[77]

The casuistical questions refer to cases which cannot be reduced to sensuous self-love. In these cases, the decision to commit suicide or to persist in life cannot be neatly divided into sensuously inspired motives for the former and morally inspired motives for the latter. The really difficult problems for the moral theorist arise in those cases where two morally inspired motives are in conflict.[78] In other words, neither maxim can be reduced to inclination.[79] One of the main problems of Kant's ethics is that he does not seem to have established any criteria for determining the priority of duties in cases of conflict. Only when moral ends are in conflict with sensuous ends has Kant established a criterion of priority. Thus Ross argues against Kant.

> We seem, then, to be in an impasse. The test of universalizability applied at one level of abstractness condemns the act; applied at another level of abstractness justifies it. And since the principle itself does not indicate at what level of abstractness it is to be applied, it does not furnish us with a criterion of the correctness of maxims, and of the rightness of acts that conform to them.[80]

This type of conflict seems to lie at the heart of the casuistical questions.

Of the five casuistical questions raised by Kant, three definately concern cases where individual interest and social interest seem to be in direct conflict: social interest seems to demand suicide whereas individual interest seems to prohibit it. Both are legitimate moral ends based on the criterion of the categorical imperative. In the first question Kant brings up the issue of martyrdom, which he defines as the sacrifice of an individual by himself for the good if other people. In the third question he raises the case of a national leader prepared to commit suicide rather than be captured alive which could result in great harm to his nation in that exhorbitant ransom demands could then be made. In the fourth question he presents the case of a person about to lose his mind from rabies,[81] an incurable disease at that time, who kills himself in order to prevent himself from infecting other people.

All these motives might be judged morally heroic by reference to the good of society. Here we have three clear examples of the type of impasse Ross attributes to Kant's ethics. It seems as though we are given no standpoint from which to determine the priority in any of these cases. Since both the individual and society are ends in themselves, it would seem that if the interest of either one is sacrificed for the other, then the sacrificed end must be reduced to the status of a means. Nevertheless, for Kant, only phenomena are means.

The third and fifth casuistical questions involve somewhat different issues. The third question concerns the possibility of permitting suicide in anticipation of an unjust death sentence, even where suicide is left open as an option by those in authority. The question here seems to be whether suicide is a legitimate means of protest against an unjust decree, a dramatic way of defying tyranny. The example given is Seneca's suicide in the wake of Nero's death sentence against him. The fifth question concerns a person deciding whether to receive a possibly fatal innoculation against disease. In Kant's time small-pox vaccination posed just such a moral problem. Is one allowed to deliberately put himself in mortal danger? One might argue that this is not truly a case of suicide, but apparently Kant believed it to be close enough to suicide to justify its inclusion in this section. Here we are faced with the problem of a conflict between the demands of the present and those of the future. Further health would seem to require innoculation; present safety would seem to forbid it. As Kant puts it: ". . . he risks his life on an uncertainty, although he does it to preserve his life." [82] In this case the person is in the very same act creating the conditions for both the possible furtherance and the possible curtailment of his life.

Ross has argued that Kant's moral theory does not provide answers for conflicts between one moral maxim and another because it does not provide a standard of application for the test of universalizability. However, we have already seen that the test of universalizability is not wholly understandable without explicating the casual constitution of a morally proposed system of nature. This casual constitution we discovered is teleological. Therefore the conflict between one moral maxim and another is not only due to a lack of a standard of application for the test of universalizability, but perhaps even more it is due to a lack of a standard for determining the priority of moral ends. This is the problem with which all of the casuistical questions deal.

The first question, concerning martydom, deals with a conflict between the moral subject as an end in himself and mankind as an end in itself. The same analysis applies in the third question concerning the willingness of a king to commit suicide in the national interest; and in the fourth question, concerning the willingness of a person with an infectious incurable disease to commit suicide in the public interest, we see the same sort of conflict. These three questions concern the conflict between the moral interest of oneself in opposition to the moral interest of other people. The second and fifth questions concern the conflict between one's moral interest in the present in opposition to one's moral interest in the future. Thus the second question concerns the conflict between one's present existence and one's protest of a coming event. The fifth question concerns the conflict between the needs of one's present existence and the needs of one's future existence, that is, future health versus present safety.

Nevertheless, all of these questions involve a basic conflict between the immediate and the remote: the first group concerns conflict between the self as an end and society as an end. The second group concerns conflict between an end *now* and an end *later*. Indeed it would seem from practical experience that the moral problems involving the most difficult soul-searching concern conflicts between moral ends themselves, rather than conflicts between authentic moral ends on the one hand and obviously immoral purposes on the other hand. When we see that the casuistical questions arise because of the lack of a standard for the application of the test of teleology, we can see that these questions are so problematic for Kant because he has not satisfactorily answered a crucial question about the locus of moral ends.

Moral ends are themselves real, even though the full realization of their projects, be they natural or social, is ideal. However, Kant has provided no criterion for determining priorities among moral ends. The categorical imperative does not help here because it can be invoked as a standard for both of the conflicting ends. Kant seems to assume that the establishment of a criterion of priority is only morally required in cases of conflict between phenomenal and noumenal factors. In these conflicts he has given us a standard for determining the exact moral locus. He has also been able to distinguish between perfect and imperfect duties. In cases of conflict between the individual and society, however, the question is: *Where* is the moral locus to be found? In the cases of conflict between the present and future interests of the person, namely, between *now* and *later,* the question is: *When* is the locus to be found?

This ambiguity concerning the locus of ends makes all five cases taken up in the casusitical questions exercises in moral reasoning for which Kant cannot provide any clear-cut answers. Their solution, it seems to me, depends on a further explication of the notion of moral end. Since Kant did not accomplish this, those philosophers who view themselves as Kantians will have to make the attempt. History has shown that the unanswered questions a philosopher has left provide a powerful stimulus for a philosophical traditon to grow up in his name. Inasmuch as Kant has inspired Kantians to follow in his philosophical footsteps, we might well consider the casuistical questions to be part of the Kantian agenda. A more collectivist interpretation of Kant, following Hegel, would opt for society over the individual in cases of conflict. On the other hand, a more individualistic interpretation of Kant, following the existentialists (for example, such diverse philosophers as Buber, Jaspers and Sartre), would opt for the individual over society in cases of conflict. Both approaches would be impossible without the background of Kant's distinction between *homo noumenon* and *homo phaenomenon*.

NOTES

¹ Trans. Louis Infield (New York: Harper Torchbooks, 1963), pp. 148-154. *Eine Vorlesung über Ethik,* ed. Paul Menzer (Berlin: Kant Gesselschaft, 1924), pp. 186-193. The *Vorlesung* was first published, posthumously, in Menzer's ed. Most scholars hold that it is a precritical work. See J. Murray's introduction to Infields trans., and P. A. Schlipp, *Kant's Pre-Critical Ethics* (Evanston, Illinois: Northwestern University Press, 1938), pp. 144-145. Cf. H. J. de Vleeschauwer, "La Doctrine du Suicide dans l'Ethique de Kant," *Kant-Studien* LVII (1966), p. 252.

² Trans. T. K. Abbott (New York: Liberal Arts Press, 1949), pp. 39-46. *Grundlegung zur Metaphysik der Sitten,* ed. Ernst Cassirer, *Kants Werke* IV (Berlin: B. Cassirer, 1922), pp. 270-280, 287.

³ Trans. L. W. Beck, The Library of Liberal Arts (Indianapolis and New York: Bobbs-Merrill, 1956), pp. 45-72. *Kritik der Praktischen Vernunft,* ed. Ernst Cassirer, *Kants Werke* V. (Berlin: B. Cassirer, 1922), pp. 50-77.

⁴ Trans. James Ellington, *The Metaphysical Principles of Virtue,* The Library of Liberal Arts (Indianapolis and New York: Bobbs-Merrill, 1964), pp. 82-85. *Metaphysik der Sitten,* ed. Ernst Cassirer, *Kants Werke* VII (Berlin: B. Cassirer, 1922), pp. 233-235.

⁵ For a discussion of the format of the *Metaphysic* see G. Anderson, "Kants Metaphysik der Sitten—ihre Idee und ihr Verhältnis zur Ethik der Wolffschen Schule," *Kant-Studien* XXVIII (1923), pp. 41-61.

⁶ See Mac Murray's introduction to Infield's trans., p. xvii.

⁷ Kant did not claim to have invented a new source of morality, but, rather, claimed to have ennunciated a new formulation of what he believed had always been the principle of morality. Thus his only claim is that of making the understanding of moral principles truly a priori. "Those who know what a formula means to a mathematician, in determining what is to be done in solving a problem without letting him go astray, will not regard a formula which will do this for all duties as something insignificant and unnecessary." *Critique of Practical Reason,* p. 8, n. 5.

⁸ See M. J. Gregor, *Laws of Freedom* (New York: Barnes and Noble, 1964), p. 128 for a discussion of this point.

⁹ "Die, wenn gleich nicht vornehmste, doch erste Pflicht des Menschen gegen sich selbst, in der Qualität seiner Tierheit, ist die Selbsterhaltung in seiner animalischen Natur." *Metaphysik der Sitten,* p. 233.

¹⁰ "Nothing can possibly be conceived in the world, or even out of it, which can be called good without qualification, except a *good will." Fundamental Principles,* p. 11. Later, Kant speaks of a good will as pertaining to "a being."

¹¹ *Fundamental Principles,* p. 39 = *Grundlegung,* p. 280. Cf. *Vorlesung,* p. 189 and Schilpp, *op. cit.,* p. 157.

¹² Paton, *The Categorical Imperative,* pp. 148, 154. Note further: "It is in the light of this attitude, common to Kant and to many of his contemporaries, that the use of the natural order as a symbol for the moral order is to be understood ... But this legitimate appeal to a systematic harmony of human purpose he may have found all the easier because he tends to regard the order of nature as itself a systematic harmony, and perhaps even a systematic harmony of purpose, however

much he may reject the claim of such beliefs to be treated as scientific knowledge."
Ibid., p. 162.

13 "Now this argument is obviously open to criticism in various ways; for instance, one might object to basing my duty on a belief about the purposiveness of nature or, less sweepingly, one might say that Kant has failed to distinguish the instinct of self-preservation (a blind tendency to preserve one's life at all costs) from the principle of self-love (a calculated desire for pleasure and aversion from pain)." J. Kemp, "Kant's Examples of the Categorical Imperative" in *Foundations of the Metaphysics of Morals with Critical Essays,* ed. R. P. Wolff, (Indianapolis and New York: Bobbs-Merrill, 1969), p. 234.

14 "Kant thus tries to make the wrongness of suicide depend on a formal self-contradiction involved in it. But where is the contradiction if self-love (i.e. the desire to get pleasure and avoid pain), which drives us to improve our condition when it can, drives a man to end his life when he cannot improve its condition?" *Kant's Ethical Theory* (New York: Oxford University Press, 1954), p. 46.

15 "Now skill in the choice of means to his own greatest well-being may be called *prudence,* in the narrowest sense. And thus the imperative which refers to the choice of means to one's own happiness, that is, the precept of prudence, is still always *hypothetical;* the action is not commanded absolutely, but only as a means to another purpose." *Fundamental Principles,* p. 33. See C. Strange, "Der Begriff der hypothetischen Imperative in der Ethik Kants," *Kant-Studien* IV (1900), pp. 232-247. Cf. G. Pätzig, "Die Logischen Formen Praktischen *Sätze* in Kants Ethik," *ibid.* LVI (1966), pp. 246-250.

16 See Bertrand Russell, *A History of Western Philosophy* (New York: Simon and Schuster, 1945), p. 711. Cf. Ross, *Kant's Ethical Theory,* pp. 32-33. Most scholars translate *Natur* as "system of nature."

17 See H. J. Paton, *The Moral Law-Kant's Groundwork of the Metaphysic of Morals* (New York: Barnes and Noble, 1958), p. 89; L. W. Beck, *Foundations of the Metaphysics of Morals of Immanuel Kant* (Indianapolis and New York: Bobbs-Merrill, 1969), p. 45.

18 "Alle praktischen Prinzipien, die ein Objekt (Materie) des Begehrungsvermögens als Bestimmungsgrund des Willens voraussetzen, sind ingesamt empirisch und können keine praktischen Gesetze abgeben." *Kritik der Praktischen Vernunft,* p. 23.

19 See *Critique of Pure Reason,* A 551 ff.

20 "What is meant by 'condition' (*Bedingung*)? Most simply we can say that it means the same as 'determination' (*Bestimmung*) in the sense of a general setting for the will ... It was his practice to call the major premise in a syllogism of the first figure a *principle* (sometimes a rule), and its middle term (the subject of the principle) he called the *condition.* In the light of this usage, we can say that 'condition' means that which is involved in the maxim as the general determination of the will." In other words, in order for the will to be able to apply the categorical imperative it must judge the nature (*Bestimmung*) of the situation where it is to be applied." L. W. Beck, *A Commentary on Kant's Critique of Practical Reason,* (Chicago: University of Chicago Press, 1960), p. 81.

21 This is best brought out in Paton's translation. "It is then seen at once that a system of nature by whose law the very same feeling whose function (*Bestimmung*) is to stimulate the furtherance of life should actually destroy life would contradict itself as consequently could not subsist as a system of nature." *The Moral Law,* p. 89.

22 See Jonathan Harrison, "Kant's Examples of the First Formulation of the

Categorical Imperative" in *Foundations of the Metaphysics of Morals with Critical Essays*, pp. 214-215.

23 On this point Kant follows Aristotle. See *Physics* 194b24 ff. See, also, Gregor, *Laws of Freedom*, p. 138.

24 Gregor, *Laws of Freedom*, p. 203.

25 Note: "Nun ist Natur im allgemeinsten Verstande die Existenz der Dinge unter Gesetzen. Die sinnliche Natur vernünftiger Wesen überhaupt ist die Existenz derselben unter empirisch bedingten Gesetzen, mithin für die Vernunft Heteronomie. Die übersinnliche Natur eben derselben Wesen ist dagegen ihre Existenz nach Gesetzen, die von alles empirischen Bedingung unabhängig sind, mithin zur Autonomie der reinen Vernunft gehören." *Kritik der Praktischen Vernunft*, p. 49. See Paton, *The Categorical Imperative*, p. 270. Cf. *Kritik der Reinen Vernunft*, B446, B485-6; and see H. J. Paton, *Kant's Metaphysic of Experience* I (London: Allen and Unwin, 1936), p. 412, n. 4.

26 "The more obvious meaning of this rule, live according to nature, is that we ought not to divert the instincts from their natural function. But the dictum, so understood, can serve as a moral principle only in so far as 'nature' also means 'human nature,' the ground of all our powers—animal, rational, and moral." Gregor, *Laws of Freedom*, p. 131. See pp. 138-139.

27 See *Critique of Practical Reason*, p. 72. Note: "Nature herself, and not merely her law, is considered a type or symbol but not as the realm of moral ends. Accordingly, Kant warns against the error of Wolff and others who confused the realm of nature and the realm of ends in their doctrine of perfection." Beck, *A Commentary on Kant's Critique of Practical Reason*, p. 162.

28 "Das Subjekt der Sittlichkeit in seiner eignen Person zernichten, ist eben so viel, als die Sittlichkeit selbst ihrer Existenz nach, so viel an ihm ist, aus der Welt vertilgen, welch doch Zweck an sich selbst ist; . . ." *Metaphysik der Sitten*, p. 234.

29 See *Kritik der Reinen Vernunft*, B369 ff.

30 *Critique of Practical Reason*, p. 45.

31 See *Grundlegung*, p. 292.

32 "Just as a schema was the 'third thing' that could mediate between pure concept and pure intuition, the type must be a third thing that can mediate between the concept of nature, all that is, and the concept of what ought to be. The third thing in the practical judgment is the concept of law itself as definitive of a realm or kingdom. Nature is phenomena under law, and natural law provides a type or model by which we can think the practical law in concreto." Beck, *A Commentary on Kant's Critique of Practical Reason*, p. 158.

33 "Nun ist der Begriff eines Wesens, das freien Willen hat der Begriff einer *causa noumenon;* und dass sich dieser Begriff nicht selbst widerspreche, davor ist man schon dadurch gesichert, dass der Begriff einer Ursache, als gänzlich vom reinen Verstande entsprungen, zugleich, auch seiner objektiven Realität in Ansehung der Gegenstände überhaupt durch die Deduktion gesichert . . ." *Kritik der Praktischen Vernunft*, p. 62. Also see Beck, *A Commentary on Kant's Critique of Practical Reason*, p. 187.

34 *Critique of Practical Reason*, p. 72.

35 Note: "The cause of which Kant speaks is the efficient or effective cause. He defines it as a cause through acting force. . . . Kant, so far as I can see, simply accepts the concepts of Newtonian physics in this connexion, and makes no attempt to alter or modify the concept of causality." Paton, *Kant's Metaphysic of Experience* II, pp. 281-282.

36 Fundamental Principles, p. 46 ". . . ob seine Handlung mit der Idee der

Menschheit, als Zweck an sich selbst, zusammen bestehen könne . . . so bedient er sich einer Person, bloss also eines Mittels . . ." *Grundlegung,* p. 287. Cf. *Vorlesung,* pp. 186-187.

37 "Der Mensch ist zwar unheilig genug, aber die Menschheit in seiner Person muss ihm heiling sein. In der ganzen Schöpfung kann alles, was man will, und worüber man etwas vermag, auch bloss als Mittel gebraucht werden; nur der Mensch, und mit ihm jedes vernünftige Geschöpf, ist Zweck an sich selbst." *Kritik der Praktischen Vernunft,* p. 96.

38 See *The Metaphysical Principles of Virtue,* pp. 83-84.

39 *Fundamental Principles,* p. 46. *Grundlegung,* pp. 287-288.

40 See Liddell and Scott, *A Greek-English Lexicon,* Vol. II, (Oxford: Clarendon Press, 1925), pp. 1772-1774. Also see Aristotle, *Physics* 194a30.

41 Book I, Chap. 10, 1100a10 ff.

42 Nevertheless, certain post-Kantian philosophers have revived the early Greek meaning of *telos.* See Martin Heidegger, *An Introduction to Metaphysics,* trans. R. Manheim (Garden City, New York: Anchor Books, 1961), pp. 49-50.

43 *Absicht* has the synonyms, *Privatzweck or subjektive Zwecke, Grundlegung,* p. 286; *relative Zwecke, ibid.; bewirkenden Zwecke, ibid.,* p. 296.

44 *Fundamental Principles,* p. 17. *Grundelgung,* p. 256.

45 Note: "The word 'causality' is commonly used by Kant in two senses. (1) It may mean 'a power to produce effects,' and (2) it may mean 'causal action . . . When he speaks of an efficient cause of being 'determined to causality' by something else, he means that it is determined to causal *action*—that it is itself caused to act causally." Paton, *The Categorical Imperative,* p. 209.

46 *Fundamental Principles,* p. 15.

47 See *Kritik der Praktischen Vernunft,* p. 96.

48 See *Ibid,* p. 25.

49 Beck, *A Commentary on Kant's Critique of Practical Reason,* p. 90, n.2.

50 See *Grundlegung,* p. 259.

51 "Our inclinations are not, by nature, law-abiding. The moral law, therefore, is felt as a contraint on them in a being possessed of practical reason. Some inclinations it thwarts by disciplining them into a coherent system . . . thus selfishness is disciplined into rational self-love." Beck, *op. cit.,* p. 219.

52 See W. Ernst, "Der Zweckbegriff bei Kant und sein Verhältnis zu den Kategorien," *Kant-Studien,* suppl. no. 14 (1909), pp. 30-31.

53 "Eben dieselbe Typik bewahrt auch vor dem Mystizismus der praktischen Vernunft welcher das, was zum *Symbol* diente, zum Schema macht, d.i. wirkliche und doch nicht sinnliche Anschauungen (eines unsichtbaren Reichs Gottes) der Anwendung der moralischen Begriffe unterlegt und ins überschwengliche hinausschweift." *Kritik der Praktischen Vernunft,* p. 78.

54 *Lectures on Ethics,* pp. 153-154. "Der Selbstmord ist aber unerlaubt und abscheulich, nicht deswegen, weil ihn Gott verboten hat, sondern Gott hat ihn verboten, weil es abscheulich ist Herabsetzung seiner innern Würde unter die Tierheit . . ." *Vorlesung,* p. 193.

55 See de Vleeschauwer, "La Doctrine du Suicide dans l'Ethique de Kant," p. 257.

56 *Critique of Pure Reason* B847, p. 664. "Wir werden, soweit praktische Vernunft uns zu führen das Recht hat, Handlungen nicht darum für Verbindlich halten, weil sie Gebote Gottes sind, *sondern sie darum als göttliche Gebote ansehen,* weil wir dazu innerlich verbindlich sind." See *Kritik der Praktischen Vernunft,* p. 140. *Kritik der Reinen Vernunft,* p. 549.

57 See *Kritik der Praktischen Vernunft*, p. 63.

58 *Critique of Judgment*, trans. J. H. Bernard (New York: Hafner Classics, 1951), pp. 285-286. See W. Frost, "Kants Teleologie," *Kant-Studien* XI (1906), p. 305.

59 See A. Trendelenburg, "Zur Geschichte des Wortes Person," ed. R. Eucken, *Kant-Studien* XIII (1908), p. 3.

60 See Paton, *The Categorical Imperative*, p. 75.

61 *The Metaphysical Principles of Virtue*, p. 83.

62 431A.

63 See *Nicomachean Ethics* 1128a5 ff.

64 *The Metaphysical Principles of Virtue*, p. 83 = *Metaphysik der Sitten*, p. 234.

65 *Ibid.*, pp. 82-83.

66 *Ibid.*, p. 84.

67 See Gregor, *Laws of Freedom*, p. 136.

68 See *Kritik der Reinen Vernunft*, A 255-256.

69 "Hence a rational being has two standpoints from which to consider himself. From both standpoints he can know the laws, this emphasis on laws should be noted, of the use of his powers and consequently the laws of all his actions. So far as he presupposes himself to belong to the sensible world, these laws are the causal laws of nature. So far as he presupposes himself to belong to the intelligent world, these laws are principles of reason which are not empirical and are independent of nature ... We need only add that it is belonging to both the sensible and the intelligible worlds that the principles on which as rational beings we should necessarily act appear to us as imperatives on which we ought to act." Paton, *The Categorical Imperative*, p. 240.

70 Kant eliminated immortality as something theoretically knowable in his critique of Mendelssohn. See *Kritik der Reinen Vernunft*, B414 ff.

71 "... als die Sittlichkeit selbst ihrer Existenz nach, so viel an ihm ist, aus der Welt vertilgen ..." *Metaphysik*, p. 234.

72 "Generally speaking, we can say that freedom is required for the establishment of the moral law itself, while the other postulates are required only for the resolution of an antinomy into which practical reason itself falls." L. W. Beck, *Critique of Practical Reason*, Introduction, p. xvii.

73 *Critique of Practical Reason*, p. 21.

74 See *Ibid.*, p. 116.

75 See *Metaphysik der Sitten*, p. 235.

76 "Casuistics is neither a science nor a part thereof; if it were, it would be a dogmatics. It is not so much a doctrine as to how something is to be found, as an exercise in how the truth is to be sought. Accordingly, it is interwoven fragmentarily and not systematically with ethics, i.e., it is added to the system like scholia." *The Metaphysical Principles of Virtue*, p. 71.

77 See Gregor, *Laws of Freedom*, pp. 101-102.

78 "For example, a hasty reader of the *Foundations*, noting Kant's harsh remarks about suicide, might conclude that Kant regards deliberately causing one's own death as wrong under all circumstances ... The point to remember is that the moral qualities of what one does are not settled by such general descriptions as 'voluntarily causing one's own death,' but rather by the maxim on which one acts." Warner Wick, introduction, *The Metaphysical Principles of Virtue*, pp. xl-xli. Cf. Gregor, *Laws of Freedom*, pp. 101-102, 135 n. 18.

79 Cf. "If—apart from all questions of duty to others—there can be a right to commit suicide, this can be justified only on the ground that there is no longer any

possibility of living a moral life and manifesting moral worth. Such a case may arise when pain is unendurable or insanity certain." Paton, *The Categorical Imperative*, p. 171. See Gregor, *Laws of Freedom*, p. 137.

[80] *Kant's Ethical Theory*, p. 33.

[81] *The Metaphysical Principles of Virtue*, p. 85. "... wagt sein Leben aufs Ungeweise: ob es war tut, um sein Leben zu erhalten ..." *Metaphysik*, p. 235.

[82] See *Grundlegung*, p. 295, n.1.

CHAPTER V

CONCLUSION

1. *Philosophy and Suicidology.*

In this study I have examined the specific prohibitions of suicide by Plato, Aquinas and Kant, as each of these philosophers rationally developed them from the general principles of his ethics. All three of these philosophers assumed that general ethical principles are both objective and intelligible, that is, that these principles are prior to any case to which they might possibly apply, and that they can be presupposed by the specific rational judgment one has to make in any particular situation.

My task has been to show how the transition from general principles to specific judgment to particular decision was accomplished by Plato, Aquinas and Kant. On this level, namely, the way the three philosophers rationally presented their arguments for the prohibition of suicide, I believe that the arguments of all three are internally cogent and not self-contradictory. Therefore, this study can be considered worthwhile if it has shown how Plato, Aquinas and Kant were able to cogently apply their general ethical principles to the specific difficulties involved in the moral judgment of suicide. I am also interested in the history of rational discussion about this problem, as a basis for further developing a position about suicide, a position which in some way will incorporate the conclusions of others, and which will take into account contemporary modes of understanding the problem of suicide.

However, neither of these purposes can be satisfied without overcoming a considerable obstacle. In the past rational discussion about suicide was philosophical; today rational discussion about suicide seems to ignore philosophy. Since the revolution in the social sciences, begun by men like Durkheim in sociology and Freud in psychology, our empirical knowledge about suicide and suicidal behavior has increased enormously. However,

115

most sociologists and psychologists have tried primarily to provide some empirically describable etiology for suicide, and then, if their interest is therapeutic as well as experimental, to propose methods for changing suicidal attitudes and suicidal behavior.

Indeed, the interest in suicide as both an empirical and a therapeutic problem, and the collection of the impressive body of data these interests have stimulated, has lead to the creation of a new inter-discipline called *suicidology,* which combines various approaches from the biological and the social sciences. However, in reading the various publications in this field I have been struck by the scarcity of philosophical discussion. Indeed, this lack of philosophical concern is apparent in that philosophical arguments which are occasionally referred to, are presented superficially, usually as illustrations of previously determined conclusions.[1]

Why is there so great a chasm between the philosophically oriented suicidology of the past and the empirically oriented suicidology of the present? The answer seems to lie in the fact that the philosophers such as Plato, Aquinas and Kant all regarded suicide as an option open to rational choice. To be sure the three differ as to which exact acts of suicide are rationally significant: Aquinas seems to be the most inclusive; Plato the most exclusive; and Kant seems to be somewhere in between. Nevertheless, all three assume that suicide can be a real possibility for rational persons: for all of us potentially; for some of us actually. None of them describes suicide as bizarre or improbable. All of them seem to be discussing a problem having immediate practical consequences. Herein lies the chasm between now and then.

The very emphasis in contemporary suicidology on empirical description and therapeutic technique seems to eliminate the factor of rational choice.[2] The assumption seems to be that *all* suicides are what Plato assumed *some* suicides to be, namely, "compelled by the occurrence of some intolerable and inevitable misfortune, . . . by falling into some disgrace that is beyond remedy or endurance."[3] It seems as though suicide is taken to be a *symptom* of something unconscious rather than the *act* of a being capable of free choice.

On the empirical level, this approach is both theoretically cogent and experimentally successful. For by bracketing the philosophical problem, if not actually denying it, sociologists and psychologists have been able to learn a great deal about the antecedent factors of suicide. For example, sociological and psychological investigations have shown that the "inevitable misfortunes," which are usually assumed by naive laymen to be external accidents "driving" certain vulnerable people to commit suicide, are actually secondary causes compared to such inner emotional states as alienation, guilt, and dependence. Thus the quest for causes has led to far more information about suicide than the use of any specifically moral principles.

Nevertheless, this type of inquiry in and of itself is not antithetical to the philosophical reflection on suicide, as long as it itself does not draw philosophical inferences from its own findings, such as: Because volition is not an empirically testable factor in the experimental study of suicide, therefore it is irrelevant in *any* understanding of suicide. Such conclusions confuse the sufficient reasons required by the empirical sciences and the necessary reasons required by moral reasoning.

Empirical information is surely indispensable for anyone who wants to reflect philosophically on any specific area of human experience. A philosophy of science would be of little value without a thorough knowledge of the actual findings of scientific research. It is a pity that so many ethicians today, who are reflecting on human action, are so ill-informed about the findings of such human sciences as sociology and psychology. Such reflection necessarily appears uninformed and superficial, and is easily dismissed as lacking in seriousness. If this is all philosophical ethics is, then journalism is probably more helpful. No, it seems clear to me that moral reasoning, although uniquely concerned with the necessary and rational reasons for human action, can never ignore the sufficient reasons as well.

If the gap between past and present suicidology were simply a question of emphasis, the former emphasizing the philosophical issues and the latter emphasizing the empirical issues, it would be easily bridgeable, for the difference in emphasis would be a methodological bracketing, a differentiation of perspectives, but nothing ultimately irreconcilable. Philosophers need empirical data for the sake of objectivity, whereas experimental scientists, being rational persons, need the questioning of philosophy in order that they might be more than manipulators of data. If this account were adequate there would be no difficulty in relating the suicidology of the past to that of the present. It would be unwarranted to use the image of a "chasm" to describe a mere difference of perspectives.

Moreover, when we come to the therapeutic side of suicidology the differences narrow. For therapy, which treats suicide as a practical human problem, cannot "bracket" philosophy. Practical judgment cannot be avoided in therapy because the therapist is not primarily interested in what factually *is*. If he were, there would be no difference between a psychologist's laboratory and a psychotherapist's treatment clinic. The therapist is only concerned with what factually *is* in that this information is an indispensable condition for what *is to be done*. The "what is to be done" is his chief therapeutic concern. Obviously, the suicidal person may or may not actually commit suicide. The therapist will attempt to influence the patient in one way or the other.

If he does nothing but describe what is going on, personally indifferent to what the practical outcome is to be,[4] then any patient who genuinely wanted to change his suicidal disposition would be best advised to save his time and money, and stay home. Surely the psychotherapist, by the very fact he is working clinically rather than experimentally, is attempting to change something; psychotherapy is rational action. If the psychotherapist is attempting to influence his patient not to commit suicide, then he himself must have already judged that suicide is something not to be done. Psychotherapy involves unavoidable moral judgments which are intrinsic to its very operation.

The question which must be answered, if the whole psychotherapeutic involvement is to have meaning, is a philosophical one. In other words, whereas the experimental psychologist stands as an outside, neutral, observer of human behavior, the clinical psychotherapist stands *within* a situation calling for a prior judgment on his own part and a subsequent judgment and decision on the part of his patient. Indeed psychotherapy can be looked upon as the process whereby a patient with the help of a therapist comes to face the various factors involved in his particular situation so that he might make a rational decision, instead of simply reacting to unconscious and unintelligible forces, as he might do without the self-scrutiny psychotherapy involves. *Nihil volitum nisi praecognitum*. Before the patient comes to a level of understanding where he can decide the *particular* question: Am I or am I not going to preserve my life?—the therapist must have already made the *specific* judgment: Life is a good to be preserved, not an evil to be destroyed.

Even if it could be argued that suicide is never the result of a rational choice—an assumption many post—Freudian and post-behaviorist psychologists would deny,[5]—the therapeutic intervention of a psychotherapist must be based on his own specific rational judgment, that is, a judgment grounded in a general metaphysical principle. Such a judgment is philosophical. Indeed, it seems to me that if Socrates were alive today, he might have compared himself to a psychotherapist rather than to a midwife. Nevertheless, the philosophical presupposition to the psychotherapeutic treatment of suicide, or any other life problem for that matter, has been largely ignored by contemporary psychotherapists.

If philosophy is so immediately relevant to the psychotherapy of the suicidal person, then why have so many therapists failed to see this relevance? The answer lies, I believe, in a fundamental misunderstanding about the nature of the relation between specific ethical judgments and particular ethical decisions.

Let me cite an example from my own experience. A young man happened to come to see me about a personal problem. Since a personal problem stems from the matrix of a whole personality, I began questioning him about his life in general. In the course of the interview he told me that his mother had attempted suicide several times and that she was currently hospitalized because of her last, almost successful, suicide attempt. As he was talking I could sense his desperation and I felt great sympathy for him. He asked me if I knew anything about suicide and suicidal people. I answered that I was very interested in the subject to the point of choosing it as the topic of my doctoral dissertation. "In clinical psychology?" he asked. "No, I replied, "in philosophy; it is about the argument presented by Plato, Aquinas and Kant for the prohibition of suicide." "Arguments!" he exclaimed. "Of what use are arguments in an actual suicide case? Could you, or Plato, or Aquinas, or Kant argue my mother out of committing suicide? If arguments would work, I would be down at the state hospital right now philosophizing with her!"

This attitude, most understandable in the desperate son of a suicidal mother, seems also to be the attitude of many psychotherapists: that because suicidal people are too desperate to respond to philosophical arguments, these arguments are of no use in the actual psychotherapeutic treatment. Indeed, they might even be harmful inasmuch as they seem to involve a cold detachment on the part of the person making them, and, as is well known to anyone who has ever tried to help a suicidal person, he is desperate for some kind of warm human contact which might save him from the self-destructive fantasies within himself. Thus many therapists are impatient with the caution and detachment of philosophy.

This *impatience,* more than anything else, explains the "chasm" between contemporary and classical suicidology. However, what is forgotten here and what surely ought to be remembered, is that the way we arrive at an ethical conclusion, that is, a free and rational practical decision, is different from the way we arrive at a theoretical conclusion, that is, an inevitable logical inference. The logical inference does not emply the participation of the one who makes it in its operation. Indeed in symbolic logic we see that the so-called "I of apperception" need not be considered in theoretically meaningful sentences.[6] However, in practical (moral) reasoning, the specific judgment implies the possible participation of the subject who makes it, and is absurd without a personal commitment. Therefore, no one can make a rationally consistent ethical judgment unless he is personally committed to following it with the appropriate particular decision should his own personal situation call for that.[7] There is no point in my making the ethical judgment: Life is to be preserved and not destroyed, unless I am committed to the particular decision: I will not commit suicide. Therefore, the so-called "cold detachment" of philosophy is a dangerous myth when applied to the process of decision-making in rational ethics.[8]

Unless the psychotherapist has himself made the specific judgment that suicide is bad, he seems to be demanding a degree of personal commitment from his patient much greater than that which he demands from himself. If the patient does not change his suicidal attitude and behavior, then the therapist has no reason for disappointment. If the patient does succeed in making the change, neither has the therapist any reason for satisfaction, for without rational grounds of action any effective instrumentality on the part of the therapist can only be good luck. It seems to be a dogma of virtually all schools of psychotherapy today that only the therapist who has confronted his own personal problems therapeutically can have enough understanding to offer direction to others in similar circumstances. Psychotherapy deals with unconscious data, to be sure. However, the judgments the therapist must make are not unconscious. Only this admission makes intelligent practical intervention possible. If only unconscious phenomena are affirmed, then we are left with an infinite regress, the removal of which is the first condition of rational action.[9]

The fact that theoretical conclusions differ from practical decisions inasmuch as theoretical judgments and intuitions differ from practical judgments and intuitions means that impersonal detachment is not required in ethical decision-making; quite the contrary, such detachment is detrimental. It we would substitute the words "philosophical *persuasion*" for "philosophical *argument*" in ethics, we would avoid the unfortunate connotation of the word "argument" which suggests to many people a sort of intellectual bullying. *Persuasion* is better suited to the specific nature of moral reasoning. Persuasion means helping the person work out his own practical decisions. One need only remember how Socrates worked with his partners in dialogue.

This subtle error which equates practical reason with theoretical reason is as much the fault of contemporary philosophers as it is of contemporary psychotherapists. For in their zeal to emulate the rigorous methods of theoretical logic they have had a tendency to ignore the specific requirements of practical reason. This tendency is most unfortunate both for ethics itself and for psychotherapy, which along with law, is perhaps most relevant for rational ethics. To paraphrase Plato: Unless philosophers become psychotherapists, or psychotherapists become philosophers, there will be no end to the problems of man.[10] Only when philosophers see that psychotherapy has immediate philosophical implications, and only when psychotherapists see that the very justification for the practice of psychotherapy itself demands philosophical intuitions, judgments, and decisions, will ethics become more than an academic game and psychotherapy become more than an intellectually suspect craft. For these reasons, the discussions of suicide and morality by Plato, Aquinas and Kant are not only examples of sound philosophical reasoning and the development of a theme in the history of ideas, but also practically important for contemporary suicidology.

2. *A Possible Unified Position.*

In my separate treatments of the three philosophers, I dealt with the internal cogency of their arguments for the prohibition of suicide. This required dealing with various objections to their arguments. Indeed, they themselves raised objections and dealt with them with great care and intellectual honesty. I also made certain comparisons between the three views of the question of suicide and related issues. I could attempt to play them off against each other, but I do not believe this would serve any good purpose, inasmuch as their respective positions are for the most part compatible, both because all three condemn suicide as immoral and because the grounds they offer for this condemnation are not antithetical. With the definite exception of Kant's reduction of *inclinatio naturalis* to the level of feeling, which is contrary to the position of Aquinas, I do not believe a contrast of the three will yield much. However, it may be helpful to sketch out a unified argument for the prohibition of suicide by synthesizing Plato, Aquinas and Kant.

Throughout this dissertation I have used for purposes of organization the descriptive structure of three relationships: that with the self, that with society, and that with God. It proved useful because all three philosophers explain their opposition to suicide in terms of these three relationships, with varying degrees of emphasis on one or another relationship in each case. It might well be helpful to contemporary suicidology, as I have outlined its needs in this chapter, to attempt to unite the most persuasive of the arguments based on each of the three relationships. In this way, this threefold structure might serve constructive as well as analytic ends.

As to the relationship with the self, which is most immediately involved in suicide, I derived several concepts from the three philosophers. From Plato came the earlier concept of the body as the protective enclosure of the soul and the later concept of the responsibility of the soul to care for the body. From Aquinas came both the concept of natural inclination and the reworking of the Augustinian concept of self-love. From Kant came the concept of self-respect or rational self-love as opposed to inclination or pathological self-love. Now inasmuch as I have attempted to show why psychotherapists must be philosophical, without sacrificing the empirical data supplied by experimental psychology, I must ask: Which of these concepts best satisfies the twofold end of internal cogency and external validity? My judgment would be in favor of the Thomistic concept of natural inclination. For this concept is the most internally cogent in that it requires the fewest presuppositions to be intelligible; and it is the most externally valid in that it alone of all the others can be seen in the unconscious factors with which suicidology must deal. Let us explore a bit more fully this judgment in favor of natural inclination.

As we saw in treating Aquinas, natural inclination can only be understood as intentionality, that is, it only has meaning when correlated with its proper object. The moral significance of natural inclination is that its object, most fundamentally, being, within the perspective of practical reason, is taken to be good. Hence natural inclination does not just intend an object, but, as seen by practical reason, it intends a *good object.* Its intentionality, therefore, is teleological. Although the practical judgment is that life is a real objective good to be consciously affirmed by the moral subject, the natural inclination which intends that good is unconscious. It lies at the very heart of the primary process we see at work even in the tiniest infant. What practical reason does then is to consciously judge as good what natural inclination has been striving for unconsciously.

What Aquinas called natural inclination psychoanalysis calls *primary process,* that is, the unconscious biological substratum of human personality. And for both it is irreducible. Therefore, both see any subsequent volitional attempt to upset primary process as inevitably destructive of human personality. The only rational program for human life, although never identical with what we might call, combining Thomistic and psychoanalytic terminology, "primary inclination," must at all times presuppose it and respect it.

Simple identification of human personality with primary inclination would be for Aquinas subhuman, for psychoanalysis psychotic. However, this presupposition of primary inclination is only possible when we are able to affirm as a general metaphysical principle: life itself is good, irrespective of subsequently bad experiences which can lead to bad patterns of living (*habitus*) which may include feelings of self-destruction. Bad *habits* are a problem for the moral education of the will in much the same way as neurosis is a problem for the psychoanalytic treatment of the ego. The affirmation of the externally good object saves natural inclination from becoming a present state of consciousness. Rational ethics, as well as psychotherapy, can only intelligently function on the basis of the affirmation of general metaphysical principles.

This is why Aquinas' notion of natural inclination has tremendous validity for contemporary suicidology. Natural inclination alone, of all the concepts of the relationship with self which have been examined, recognizes that the sources of human vitality are unconscious and that practical reason affirms what nature intends. Psychoanalysis has convincingly shown, I believe, that the suicidal person is not suffering from a drive of his immortal soul to escape the confines of his mortal body, nor a sensual desire to ignore moral duty, but rather from inner alienation from the biological sources of his whole personality and from a desire to dominate nature by will. Thus the close connection between repression, especially sexual repression, and suicidal feelings can be seen in their identical denial of natural inclination.[11]

What Aquinas' concept of natural inclination does for psychotherapeutic suicidology is to philosophically explicate its own fundamental presuppositions. Without the philosophical affirmation, "Life is a good to be pursued," the real priority of primary process cannot be consistently maintained. It becomes, rather, a mere intellectual construct.

As to the relationship with society which is involved in suicide because man is a social being, we derived several concepts from the three philosophers. From Plato came the concept of social responsibility. From Aquinas came the concept of social participation, based largely on Aristotle. From Kant came the concept of the ideal realm of ends.

I believe that the social dimension of suicide is even more important than the individual dimension, because it concerns that area of life in which man is most consciously and presently involved and in which, therefore, the specifically human properties of intellect and will are involved to the greatest extent. Only in society is man involved in uniquely human relationships. Other beings have natural inclinations and other beings can be seen as creatures of God, but society can not be seen as the arena of discursive dialogue apart from human participation.[12]

Of the three philosophers, Plato, more than any other, has most fully developed his social philosophy. He, to a far greater extent than the other two, has shown that social participation is required by the very operation of human reason, for dialectic, its very apex, is impossible without real interpersonal discourse, without dialogue. Because of this need for dialogue, the rational person cannot transcend his social ties in order to attain a higher level of existence: reason is co-equal with authentic sociality.

This point has tremendous significance for suicidology, for the unconscious conflicts which give rise to the suicidal situation seem to involve interpersonal crises much more than they involve the simple repression of primary process. The phenomena of guilt and self-punishment are not explained on the basis of natural inclination alone, because they presuppose interpersonal interaction. They require an understanding of the history of the patient, a history which is social since it involves his interactions with significant other persons in his lifetime. And, as Harry Stack Sullivan showed (contrary to Freud), interpersonal relationships cannot be reduced to functions of biological needs.[13] Plato anticipated this view when he saw the philosophical city as culminating in the exercise of dialectic which works through dialogue, through rational discourse.

For Plato the temptation of the philosopher, the rational person, is to take his leave of human society when he believes that having received all that it can give him, he can attain more in an ideal world which transcends human society. Plato's answer is that one cannot transcend society in the name of self-perfection without simultaneously denying the necessary context for self-perfection. This point is of immense import for contemporary suicidology in that the loneliness and social alienation of the suicidal person are basic factors in his self-destructive outlook. Therefore, psychotherapy must begin a process of resocialization, a process by which the patient can discover self-fulfilling goals within interpersonal interaction, within society.

Both Aquinas and Kant recognized the moral significance of man's sociality, but Plato, to a far deeper extent then either of them, showed how a society worthy of human loyalty must be discursively constituted. Therefore, one cannot abandon society by committing suicide on the basis of a seemingly rational judgment; Plato has shown that authentic reason cannot be either antisocial or asocial. And Plato, with his rich literary gift, emphasizes the schizoid anti-sociality manifest in suicide by proposing that the body of the one committing suicide be buried in an isolated, unmarked, grave, which is obviously symbolic of the social alienation he has chosen to act out by committing suicide.

The very fact that psychotherapy consists of a dialogue between therapist and patient, and the concept of transference indicates that this dialogue includes all the meaningful human relationships in the life of the patient,[14] means that we are dealing with the discursively constituted society of which Plato spoke. Psychotherapy itself is a social phenomenon. Thus the social significance of suicide is of immediate import in the psychotherapeutic treatment of the suicidal person. Here again suicidology needs philosophy, because if the prior value of society for the human person is not understood, its priority to any individual state of affairs (such as suicidal feelings) cannot be consistently maintained. Why society as a human good is intended by human sociality must be intelligible to us before we can present resocialization as an intelligent option for the rational person.

As to the relationship with God the significance of the arguments of Plato, Aquinas and Kant is more difficult to ascertain. First, it is very doubtful that Kant prohibits suicide on the basis of a real relationship with God. For Kant, God merely confirms a morality already constituted on the basis of man's autonomy as a moral being. As for Plato and Aquinas, who do prohibit suicide on the basis of a real relationship with God, contemporary suicidology does not assume a specifically theological dimension, unless of course religious persons having problems with suicidal feelings come to a clergyman expecting a theological approach to the resolution of these problems. However, this possibility gets one into the area of revelation and the theologies or particular faith-communities. Suicidology, on the other hand, in its attempt to be universally acceptable, cannot work on faith assumptions, because there would then have to be as many suicidologies as there are theologies.

In my own theological outlook a positive relationship with God, that is, one involving real presence and not just inference, can only take place within the framework of revelation as affirmed by a faith-community in history. Therefore, I believe that it would be a meaningless to attempt to ground the prohibition of suicide in God's lordship, unless there were a prior affirmation of those revelatory events by which that lordship was made manifest to a particular community, and by which the community constituted its very identity on the sole basis of the acceptance of that revelation.

The most that human reason can accomplish, in this context, is to develop a *via negativa,* namely, to rationally refute any theory of human nature or action which would posit the impossibility of the revealed authority of God operating in human existence. In the theoretical sphere this method would include the refutation of such theories as atheism and pantheism on the basis of their own claims. In the practical sphere this method would include the rejection of acts such as suicide which assume that the human person has total authority over his own life.

Nevertheless, it is important to remember that Plato, Aquinas and Kant deal with the question of suicide not so much in terms of the nature of God or revelation, but rather, in terms of human nature in relation to transcendence. Their primary problem in this context is not the notion that one is the property of his creator. Their concern is much more with the human attempt to transcend bodily finitude, which justifies itself as flight away from the limited world towards an exclusive relationship with the limitless God.

If one believes there is something better beyond the grave, then why not take matters into his own hands? This sort of problem, not uncommon among certain suicidal psychotics, is not exclusively theological in the dogmatic sense, but is essentially anthropological.

Plato, Aquinas and Kant recognized this in that they all dealt with the problem more in terms of the limitations of human knowledge than in terms of the authority of God. Rational choice and action are only possible on the basis of real knowledge. The very limitation inherent in human reason itself makes such a suicide an essentially irrational act. Human reason cannot intelligently operate unless its range of operation is clearly delineated. One must identify what is unknowable and understand why it is unknowable.

Even an agnostic, in order to function intelligently, must acknowledge the finite limits of his own rational powers. He must accept the fact that he is a human and not God, whether he believes God is real or only imaginary. If theology must deny that man has concrete knowledge of what lies beyond the grave, then certainly secular suicidology must refute any such claims on the part of suicidal persons. Therefore, the finite limitations on man as a rational being, which Plato, Aquinas and Kant explicated, is meaningful for suicidology even if neither the patient nor the therapist is religious. All these philosophers hold that man is not only limited by something transcendent, but that man is also limited by something immanent, by his own finite nature.

One manifestation of this immanent limitation is one's ignorance of what there is for him after death. Kant, more than Plato or Aquinas, I think, was best able to refute this type of suicidal "logic" in that he drew a very clear and consistent distinction between the function of grounds and postulates in moral reason. In my own theological outlook, which is a reflection of the revelation accepted by my own particular faith-community, the doctrine of life after death is a theological postulate. It is a theoretical affirmation required by a full understanding of the primary religious reality, just as Kant held it to be a postulate required by a full understanding of the primary moral reality. The logic is analogous.

Perhaps this notion of the intrinsic limitedness of man, a notion which I think Kant most convincingly developed, might be the most important point philosophy can contribute to suicidology. Suicide is egocentric narcissism in its most radical manifestation. It is the most desperate human attempt to be a complete universe unto oneself. The suicidal person must be patiently taught to see and accept his own limitations so that he can affirm a world outside himself; only thus can he be helped to draw vitality once again from natural inclination, to converse with other persons, and to be silent in the face of what he cannot know, which for some is to wait for God.[15]

NOTES

[1] For example, in the most philosophically oriented book on the subject I could find, *On the Nature of Suicide,* ed. E. S. Shneidman (San Francisco: Jossey Bass, 1969), the most philosophical statement it contained was: "... the possibilities of suicide will always oppose psychiatry's efforts to rid itself of metaphysical concern, for once that possibility disrupts the civilized and ordinary boundaries of psychotherapy, every technical category loses its ordinary place in our thinking and must be questioned with a new urgency..." Leslie H. Faber, "The Phenomenology of Suicide," *ibid.,* p. 104. However, this statement is not in any way logically developed.

[2] See, e.g., Don D. Jackson, "Theories of Suicide" in *Clues to Suicide,* ed. E. S. Shneidman and N. L. Farberow (New York: McGraw-Hill, 1957), p. 11.

[3] *Laws* 873C.

[4] In current psychiatric thinking this is called "non-directive therapy."

[5] For a critique of Freud and Behaviorism for their elimination of considerations of will in psychotherapy, see Rollo May, *Love and Will* (New York: W. W. Norton, 1969), pp. 194-208.

[6] See Bertrand Russell, *An Inquiry into Meaning and Truth* (Baltimore: Penguin Books, 1962), pp. 102 ff.

[7] See R. M. Hare, *Freedom and Reason* (Oxford: The Clarendon Press, 1963), p. 73.

[8] Note Maritain, *Existence and the Existent,* p. 61, n.3, who in describing what he calls the "practico-practical syllogism" writes: "The following is an example of the second syllogism: 'Murder is forbidden by the law. This act which attracts me is murder, *and would cause me to deviate from what I love best.* Therefore *I shall not do it* (and long live law!) ... In the second syllogism it is the existential disposition of the subject in the free affirmation of his unique self which decides the question."

[9] See Aristotle, *Nicomachean Ethics* 1109b30-1110a40.

[10] Cf. *Republic* 474A.

[11] See "Psychopathology of Everyday Life" in *The Basic Writings of Sigmund Freud,* ed. and trans. A. A. Brill (New York: Random House, 1938), pp. 123-128.

[12] See Aristotle, *Politics* 1253 a 5-20.

[13] See "The Interpersonal Theory of Mental Disorder" in *The Collected Works of Harry Stack Sullivan* II, ed. H. S. Perry, M. L. Gawel, and M. Gibson (New York: W. W. Norton, 1956), pp. 3-11. For the application of Sullivan's theories to the treatment of suicide, see Maurice R. Green, "Suicide: The Sullivanian Point of View" in *The Cry for Help,* ed. N. L. Farberow and E. S. Schneidman (New York, Toronto and London: McGraw-Hill, 1961), pp. 220-235.

[14] See Freud, *The Origin and Development of Psychoanalysis,* Gateway ed. (Regnery, Chicago, 1955), pp. 62-69.

[15] "No eye hath seen but Thine o'God what Thou wilt do for those who wait for Thee." Isaiah 64:3 according to the interpretation in Babylonian Talmud, *Tractate Abodah Zarah,* folio 65a.

BIBLIOGRAPHY

Adler, Mortimer. *The Time of Our Lives.* New York: Holt, Rinehart and Winston, 1970.

Anderson, G. "Kants Metaphysik der Sitten—ihre Idee und ihr Verhältnis zur Ethik der Wolffschen Schule," *Kant-Studien,* Vol. 28, (1923), pp. 41-61.

Aristotle. *Metaphysics,* 2 Vols. Ed. and trans. Hugh Tredennick, Loeb Classical Library. Harvard University Press, 1933.

―――. *Nicomachean Ethics,* Ed. and trans. H. Rackham, Loeb Classical Library. Harvard University Press, 1926.

―――. *Physics,* 2 Vols. Ed. and trans. Philip Wicksteed and F. M. Cornford, Loeb Classical Library. Harvard University Press, 1929.

―――. *Politics,* Ed. and trans. H. Rackham, Loeb Classical Library. Harvard University Press, 1932.

Armstrong, R. A. *Primary and Secondary Precepts in Thomistic Natural Law Teaching.* The Hague; M. Nijhoff, 1966.

Augustine. *City of God,* Vol. I, Ed. and trans. G. E. McCracken, Loeb Classical Library. Harvard University Press, 1957.

―――. *On Free Will,* Trans. Richard McKeon in *Selections From Medieval Philosophers,* Vol. I, Ed. R. McKeon. New York: Charles Scribner's Sons, 1929, pp. 11-64.

―――. *On the Trinity,* Trans. A. W. Haddan, rev. G. T. Shedd, in *The Basic Writings of Saint Augustine,* Vol. II, Ed. W. J. Oates. New York: Random House, 1948, pp. 667-878.

Beck, Lewis White. *A Commentary on Kant's Critique of Practical Reason.* University of Chicago Press, 1960.

Bluck, R. S. *Plato's Life and Thought.* London: Routledge and Kegan Paul, 1949.

Bourke, Vernon J. *St. Thomas and the Greek Moralists.* Milwaukee: Marquette University Press, 1947.

Buckley, Joseph. *Man's Last End.* St. Louis and London: B. Herder, 1949.

Cornford, F. M. *Plato's Cosmology.* London: Routledge and Kegan Paul, 1937.

Crombie, I. M. *An Examination of Plato's Doctrines,* Vol. I. London: Routledge and Kegan Paul, 1962.

Demos, Raphael. *The Philosophy of Plato.* New York: Chas. Scribner's Sons, 1939.

de Vleeschauwer, H. J. "La Doctrine du Suicide dans l'Ethique de Kant," *Kant-Studien,* Vol. 57 (1966), 251-265.

Durkheim, Emile. *Suicide,* Trans. J. J. Spaulding and George Simpson. Glencoe, Ill.: The Free Press, 1951.

Epictetus. *Discourses,* Trans. P. E. Matheson, in *The Stoic and Epicurean Philosophers,* ed., W. J. Oates. New York: Random House, 1940, pp. 224-484.

Ernst, W. "Der Zweckbegriff bei Kant und sein Verhältnis zu den Katagorien," *Kant-Studien,* Supp. no. 14 (1909).

Farber, Leslie H. "The Phenomenology of Suicide," in *On the Nature of Suicide,* ed., E. S. Shneidman. San Francisco: Jossey-Bass, 1969, pp. 102-113.

Farrell, Walter. *A Companion to the Summa,* 3 Vols. New York: Sheed and Ward, 1940.

Feibleman, J. K. *Religious Platonism.* London: Allen and Unwin, 1959.

Frank, Erich. *Plato und die Sogenannten Pythägorer,* Halle: Niemayer, 1923.

Friedländer, Paul. *Platon,* Vol. III. Berlin: Walter de Gruyter, 1960.

Freud, Sigmund. *Beyond the Pleasure Principle,* Trans. James Strachy. New York: Bantam Books, 1959.

————. *The Origin and Development of Psychoanalysis.* Gateway ed., Chicago: Regnery, 1955.

————. "The Psychopathology of Everyday Life," in *The Basic Writings of Sigmund Freud,* ed. and trans. A. A. Brill. New York: Random House, 1938.

Frost, W. "Kants Teleologie," *Kant-Studien,* Vol. II (1906), pp. 297-347.

Gilson, Étienne. *God and Philosophy.* Yale University Press, 1941.

————. *Moral Values and the Moral Life,* Trans. L. R. Ward. St. Louis and London: B. Herder, 1931.

————. *Le Thomisme,* 5th ed., Paris: J. Vrin, 1947.

Green, Maurice R. "Suicide—The Sullivanian Point of View," in *The Cry for Help,* ed. N. L. Farberow and E. S. Shneidman. New York, Toronto and London: McGraw-Hill, 1961, pp. 220-235.

Gregor, Mary J. *Laws of Freedom.* New York: Barnes and Noble, 1964.

Grisez, Germain G. "The First Principle of Practical Reason," *Natural Law Forum,* Vol. 10 (1965), pp. 168-201.

Gustafson, G. J. *The Theory of Natural Appetency in the Philosophy of St. Thomas.* Washington: Catholic University Press, 1944.

Hare, R. M. *Freedom and Reason.* Oxford: Clarendon Press, 1963.

Harrison, Jonathan. "Kant's Examples of the First Formulation of the Categorical Imperative," in *Foundations of the Metaphysics of Morals with Critical Essays,* ed. R. P. Wolff. Indianapolis and New York: Bobbs-Merrill, 1969.

Heidegger, Martin. *An Introduction to Metaphysics,* Trans. R. Manheim. Garden City, New York: Doubleday, Anchor Books, 1961.

————. *The Holy Scriptures,* New York, New York: Hebrew Publishing Co., 1950.

Hook, Sidney. "The Ethics of Suicide," *International Journal of Ethics,* Vol. 37 (1927), pp. 173-188.

Hume, David. "Essay on Suicide," in Raziel Abelson, *Ethics and Metaethics*. New York: Martin's Press, 1963, pp. 108-116.

Jackson, Don D. "Theories of Suicide," in *Clues to Suicide* ed. E. S. Shneidman and N. L. Farberow. New York, Toronto and London: McGraw-Hill, 1957, pp. 11-21.

Jaffa, Harry V. *Thomism and Aristotelianism*. University of Chicago Press, 1952.

Kant, Immanuel. *Grundlegung zur Metaphysik der Sitten*, ed. Ernst Cassirer, ... *Kants Werke*, Vol. IV. Berlin: B. Cassirer, 1922.

————. *Foundations of the Metaphysics of Morals*, Trans. L. W. Beck. Indianapolis and New York: Bobbs-Merrill, 1969.

————. *Fundamental Principles of the Metaphysic of Moral*, trans. T. K. Abbott. New York: Liberal Arts Press, 1949.

————. *The Moral Law—Kant's Groundwork of the Metaphysic of Morals*, trans. H. J. Paton. New York: Barnes and Noble, 1958.

————. *Kritik der Praktischen Vernunft*, ed. Ernst Cassirer, *Kants Werke*, Vo. V. Berlin: B. Cassirer, 1922.

————. *Critique of Practical Reason*, The Library of Liberal Arts, trans. and into. L. W. Beck. Indianapolis and New York: Bobbs-Merrill, 1956.

————. *Kritik der Reinen Vernunft*, ed. Ernst Cassirer, *Kants Werke*, Vol. III. Berlin: B. Cassirer, 1922.

————. *Critique of Pure Reason*, trans. Norman Kemp Smith. New York: St. Martin's Press, 1965.

————. *Metaphysik der Sitten*, ed. Ernst Cassirer, *Kants Werke*, Vol. VII. Berlin: B. Cassirer, 1922.

————. *The Metaphysical Principles of Virtue*, The Library of Liberal Arts, trans. James Ellington, intro. Warner Wick. Indianapolis and New York: Bobbs-Merrill, 1964.

————. *Kritik der Urteilskraft*, ed. Ernst Cassirer, *Kants Werke*, Vol. V. Berlin: B. Cassirer, 1922.

————. *Critique of Judgment*, trans. J. H. Bernard. New York: Hafner Classics. 1951.

————. *Eine Vorlesung über Ethik*, ed. Paul Menzer, Berlin: Kant-Gesellschaft, 1924.

————. *Lectures on Ethics*, trans. Louis Infield, intro. J. MacMurray. New York: Harper Torchbooks, 1963.

Kemp, J. "Kant's Examples of the Categorical Imperative," in *Foundations of the Metaphysics of Morals with Critical Essays*, ed. R. P. Wolff, pp. 230-244.

Liddell, H. G. and Scott, Robert. *A Greek-English Lexicon*, 2 Vols. rev. ed. Oxford: The Clarendon Press, 1925.

Lottin, Dom Odon: *Le Droit Naturel chez Saint Thomas et sés Prédécesseurs*, 2nd rev. ed. Bruges: Beyaert, 1931.

Lovejoy, Arthur O. *The Great Chain of Being*. New York: Harper Torch Books, 1960.

132

SUICIDE AND MORALITY

May, Rollo. *Love and Will.* New York: W. W. Norton, 1969.
Maritain, Jacques. *Existence and the Existent,* trans. Lewis Galantiere and G. B. Phelan, Image Books, Garden City, New York, 1957.
———. *Man and the State.* University of Chicago Press, 1951.
———. *The Person and the Common Good,* trans. J. J. Fitzgerald. New York: Chas. Scribner's Sons, 1947.
Monahan, W. B. *The Moral Theology of St. Thomas Aquinas,* Vol. I. London: Baylis and Son, 1942.
More, P. E. *The Religion of Plato.* Princeton University Press, 1921.
Mueller, Gustav E. "Plato and the Gods," *Philosophical Review,* Vol. 45 (Summer, 1936), pp. 457-472.
Muller, C. "Die Methode einer Reinen Ethik," *Kant-Studien,* Supp. no. 11 (1908).
Murray, John Courtney. *We Hold These Truths.* New York: Sheed and Ward, 1960.
Naus, John E. *The Nature of the Practical Intellect According to St. Thomas Aquinas.* Rome: Gregorian University, 1959.
———. *The New Testament,* trans. E. J. Goodspeed, University of Chicago Press, 1923.
Nietzsche, Friedrich. *Zur Genealogie der Moral.* Munich: Carl Haner Verlag, 1967.
Novak, David. *Law and Theology in Judaism.* New York: KTAV, 1974.
O'Connor, D. J. *Aquinas and Natural Law.* New York: Macmillan, 1967.
O'Sullivan, Richard. "The Ethics of Suicide—Aquinas and the Common Law," *The Catholic Lawyer,* Vol. II (1956), pp. 146-148.
Paton, H. J. *The Categorical Imperative,* University of Chicago Press, 1948.
———. *Kant's Metaphysic of Experience,* 2 Vols. London: Allen and Unwin, 1936.
Pätzig, G. "Die Logischen Formen Praktischen Satze in Kant's Ethik," *Kant-Studien,* Vol. 56 (1966), pp. 237-252.
Philo. *Allegories,* Vol. I, ed. and trans. G. H. Whitaker, Loeb Classical Library, Harvard University Press, 1929.
Plato. *Apology, Crito, Euthyphro, Phaedo, Phaedrus,* ed. and trans. H. N. Fowler, Loeb Classical Library, Harvard University Press, 1914.
———. *Cratylus,* ed. and trans. H. N. Fowler, Loeb Classical Library, Harvard University Press, 1926.
———. *Laws,* 2 Vols., ed. and trans. R. G. Bury, Loeb Classical Library, Harvard University Press, 1926.
———. *Laws,* 2 Vols., ed. and comm. E. B. England, Manchester University Press, 1921.
———. *Menexenus,* ed. and trans. R. G. Bury, Loeb Classical Library, Harvard University Press, 1929.
———. *Phaedo,* ed. and notes R. D. Archer-Hind. New York: Macmillan, 1894.
———. *Plato's Phaedo,* trans. and comm. R. S. Bluck. Indianapolis and New York: Bobbs Merrill, 1955.

————. *Plato's Phaedo,* trans. and comm. R. Hackforth, Cambridge University Press, 1955.

————. *Philebus,* ed. and trans. W. R. M. Lamb, Loeb Classical Library, Harvard University Press, 1925.

————. *Protagoras,* ed. and trans. W. R. M. Lamb, Loeb Classical Library, Harvard University Press, 1924.

————. *The Republic of Plato,* trans. and comm. F. M. Cornford. New York: Oxford University Press, 1945.

————. *Republic,* 2 Vols., ed. and trans. Paul Shorey, Loeb Classical Library, Harvard University Press, 1937.

————. *Sophist, Theaetetus,* ed. and trans. H. N. Fowler, Loeb Classical Library, Harvard University Press, 1921.

————. *Symposium,* ed. and trans. W. R. M. Lamb, Loeb Classical Library, Harvard University Press, 1925.

————. *Timaeus,* ed. and trans. R. G. Bury, Loeb Classical Library, Harvard University Press, 1929.

Plotinus. *Enneads,* 3 Vols., ed. and trans. A. H. Armstrong, Loeb Classical Library, Harvard University Press, 1966.

Rommen, Heinrich A. *The Natural Law,* trans. T. R. Hanley, B. Herder, St. Louis and London, 1947.

Ross, W. D. *Aristotle.* New York: Meridian Books, 1960.

————. *Kant's Ethical Theory.* New York: Oxford University Press, 1954.

Russell, Bertrand. *A History of Western Philosophy.* New York: Simon and Schuster, 1945.

————. *An Inquiry into Meaning and Truth.* Baltimore: Penguin Books, 1962.

Rutenber, C. G. *The Doctrine of the Imitation of God in Plato.* New York: King's Crown Press, 1946.

Sartre, Jean-Paul. *Being and Nothingness,* trans. Hazel Barnes. New York: Philosophical Library, 1956.

Schilpp, Paul A. *Kant's Pre-Critical Ethics.* Evanston, Illinois: Northwestern University Press, 1938.

Seneca. *Epistolae,* Vol. III, ed. and trans. R. M. Gummere, Loeb Classical Library, Harvard University Press, 1925.

Sertillanges, A. P. *La Philosophie Morale de Saint Thomas d'Aquin,* rev. ed., 1946.

Simon, Yves R. *A General Theory of Authority.* South Bend, Indiana: University of Notre Dame Press, 1962.

————. *Philosophy of Democratic Government,* University of Chicago Press, 1951.

Skemp, J. B. *The Theory of Motion in Plato's Later Dialogues,* Cambridge University Press, 1942.

Solmsen, Friedrich. *Plato's Theology,* Cornell University Press, 1942.

Stange, C. "Der Begriff der Hypothetischen Imperative in der Ethik Kants," *Kant-Studien,* Vol. IV (1900), pp. 232-247.

Strauss, Leo. *Natural Right and History,* University of Chicago Press, 1953.

134 SUICIDE AND MORALITY

Sullivan, Harry Stack. "The Interpersonal Theory of Mental Disorder," in *The Collected Works of Harry Stack Sullivan*, ed. H. S. Perry, M. L. Gawel, M. Gibbon, New York: W. W. Norton, 1956, Vol. II, pp. 3-11.

Táran, Leonardo. "Plato, Phaedo 62A," *American Journal of Philology*, Vol. 87 (July, 1966), pp. 326-336.

Taylor, A. E. *Plato—The Man and His Work*. Edinburgh: Morrison and Gibb, 1927.

Thiry, Leon. "The Ethical Theory of Saint Thomas," *Journal of Religion*, Vol. 50, no. 2 (April, 1970), pp. 169-185.

Thomas Aquinas. *The Basic Writings of St. Thomas Aquinas*, 2 Vols. trans. and notes Anton C. Pegis. New York: Random House, 1945.

————. *In Libros Ethicorum*, ed. R. M. Spiazzi. Rome: Marietti, 1964.

————. *Commentary on Nicomachean Ethics*, 2 Vols. trans. C. I. Litzinger, Chicago: Regnery, 1964.

————. *Opera*, 34 vols., ed. P. Fiaccadori, Parma, 1852-1873.

————. *De Regium Principium*, ed. Taurini, Rome: Marietti, 1948.

————. *Summa Theologiae*, 3 vols., ed. P. Caramello, Rome: Marietti, 1962.

————. *Summa Theologica*, 15 vols., trans. the Fathers of the English Dominican Province, London: Burnes, Oates and Washbourne, Ltd., 1922.

————. *Truth*, 3 vols. trans. R. W. Schmidt, S. J., Chicago: Regnery, 1954.

Babylonian Talmud, Romm ed. Vilna, 1898, Vol. XVI.

Trendelenburg, A. "Zur Geschichte des Wortes Person," ed. R. Eucken, *Kant-Studien*, Vol. 13 (1908), pp. 1-17.

van Camp, J. and Canart, Paul. *Le Sens du Mot Theios chez Platon*. Louvain, 1956.

von Wilamowitz-Moellendorf, Ulrich. *Platon*, Vol. I., Berlin: Weidmann, 1929.

White, William Alanson, *Forty Years of Psychiatry*. Washington and New York: Nervous and Mental Diseases Publishing Co., 1933.

Wild, John. *Plato's Theory of Man*. Harvard University Press, 1946.

Wolff, Hans M. *Plato—Der Kampf ums Sein*, Bern: Francke Verlag, 1951.

Wolfson, Harry Austryn. *Philo*, 2 vols. Harvard University Press, 1947.

INDEX

135